THE NEW
ANCIENT COI

Based on

Ancient Collects

and Other Prayers
Selected for Devotional Use
from Various Rituals;

by

William Bright

Completely Revised and
Refreshed

by

Paul C. Stratman

2017.

This work is based on *Ancient Collects and Other Prayers: Selected for Devotional Use from Various Rituals; with an Appendix on the Collects in the Prayer-book* by William Bright, Sixth edition, London: Parker and Co., 1887. This work is in the public domain.

1

Contact information:

Paul C. Stratman
1000 Mary Street
Beaver Dam, WI 53916
pcstratman@gmail.com
acollectionofprayers.wordpress.com

This book is printed in Linux Libertine 11 pt

DEDICATION

To the glory of God alone
for his rich *grace*,
and with thanks

to my parents
who first taught me
the Christian *faith*,

and to all the teachers
in the schools of my church
who gave me a firm foundation in *Scripture*.

PREFACE TO THE NEW ANCIENT COLLECTS
by Paul C. Stratman, S. T. M.

ALMIGHTY God,
every good prayer comes from you,
and you pour out
the Spirit of grace and prayer
on all who desire it.
Deliver us from cold hearts
and wandering minds
when we draw near you,
that with steadfast thoughts
and warmed affections
we may worship you in spirit and in truth;
through Jesus Christ our Lord.

William Bright, revised, #579

SINCE the Second Vatican Council and the publication of *Lutheran Book of Worship* (1978), the American revision of *The Book of Common Prayer* (1979) and *The Alternative Service Book* of the Church of England (1980), the use of traditional liturgical English in Christian worship has almost disappeared from all English-speaking Christian denominations. In my opinion, an update of language isn't just a matter of relevance, it's a matter of clarity. People haven't spoken in the English of the 1600s since... the 1600s. To use 1600s English in worship is to speak a foreign language. St. Paul wrote, *"in the church I would rather speak five intelligible words to instruct others than ten thousand words in a tongue"* (1 Corinthians 14:19 NIV).

At the same time, there is great value in hearing and using the prayers of Christians who have lived, sweated and prayed throughout the centuries. When we confess, "I believe in the holy Christian church, the communion of saints," we are confessing a fellowship that goes beyond time, national borders, and even beyond denominations and traditions.

Bright's *Ancient Collects* presents us with this challenge: Here is a treasury of some of the best prayers from the history of Christendom, selected by William Bright (1824-1901), the Christian scholar and historian. Each prayer is a treasure for its historic value and also a treasure for its content—but the content is in an English that no one really speaks and that few can understand without considerable work. In Bright's *Ancient Collects,* we have words that are understandable but out of common use, *thee, thou, thy;* and older forms of words: *comest, lovest;* we have words that need constant explanation: *vouchsafe, benignantly, succor;* words that just seem odd: *wherinsoever* (p. 12.1), and some words that have a completely different meaning to the modern ear than to the classical ear: *awful* (p. 129.2), *intercourse* (p. 54.1, 175.2, heading), *holy bosoms* (p. 70.1)! Traditional liturgical English also was not very economic. "Grant, we beseech Thee, almighty God, that Thou wouldst vouchsafe unto us Thy bounty" can be rendered with about a quarter of the words. "Almighty God, bless us." Is the meaning clarified? Absolutely. Is some beauty lost? Perhaps, but that can be compensated by a use of dignified English and by letting the beauty of the meaning of the prayer shine through.

We live in a time when the meaning of everything is questioned—even to the point where some say that nothing has any meaning (postmodernism). These prayers do have meaning. They came from the hearts of sincere Christians of the past as they were speaking to their God and Savior. Since this revision is about preserving and paying attention to the meaning of the prayers, I tried to *preserve the meaning* of all the prayers in dignified, contemporary liturgical English with a few more liberties than William Bright allowed himself.

Three different types of revision were done:
1) Some prayers got a *simple mending*. *Thee, thou* and *thy* were replaced with *you* and *your; comest* and *livest* and *reignest* were replaced with *comes, lives* and *reigns,* etc., and if nothing more than that was needed, nothing more was done.
2) Some prayers needed to be *translated* from traditional liturgical English to contemporary liturgical English. The simple mending described above was done, but more obscure words had to be replaced with new words or sometimes replaced with short phrases. Classical writing often put the most important words at the beginning of a sentence for emphasis—which can be confusing for a modern reader—so words and phrases were moved for clarity. Sometimes a redundancy was removed if the repetition added little to the prayer. Since I saw this kind of revision as translation, I took care to keep the same meaning as Bright's translations.
3) Some prayers, especially the longer ones, had so many redundancies and so many words that needed to be replaced that the process of rendering the prayer became more of a *paraphrase.*

Along with language, there is another problem in Bright's *Ancient Collects*—a problem that William Bright himself was aware of. In Bright's original preface, he stated that he took few liberties in translating, and that it was especially challenging in translating words relating to *merit* and *reward*:

The often-recurring word *mereamur* has not been rendered "may deserve" or "may merit," because those verbs would convey a false notion of the original, making it express the doctrine of "condignity;" but by such words as "may obtain," or "may be enabled to have;" not by any means with a wish to ignore the fact, that it also sometimes implies the being "fitted" to obtain, and sometimes being "rewarded" with.

The issues of *merit* and *reward* are deeply connected with *sanctification.* Are we sanctified in this life, that is, made holy to the point where we are *fit for heaven?* Yes and no. On the one hand, sanctification as a matter of *status* is already complete. *"Christ loved the church and gave himself up for her, that he might sanctify her, having cleansed her by the washing of water with the word"* (Ephesians 5:25). On the other hand, sanctification as a *process of growth* is never complete. *"Grow in the grace and knowledge of our Lord and Savior Jesus Christ."* (2 Peter 3:18).

I also found other doctrinal issues in some of the prayers. The *condignity, merit, reward* and *sanctification* problems mentioned above, along with the confusion of *sacramental* with *sacrificial* would make the prayers useful to fewer Christians, so some change in *meaning* was made. Still, I tried to do as little change as possible to try to keep the integrity and most of the meaning of the prayer intact. When I felt additions or changes of meaning were significant enough, I put a footnote with notice of the addition, or with Bright's unmodified line (noted with "Original translation"). Each prayer has a page number reference for all editions and reprints of Bright's *Ancient Collects* since the third edition, and Bright's references to the original ancient sources.

For these reasons, I am sure some, perhaps many will say, "What have you done to Bright's *Ancient Collects?* You've stripped all the beauty out of the language and twisted the meaning to your own theological tastes." You can still go to Amazon.com and order a copy of the original, or read it online at Google Books. My hope (and prayer) with this revision is that with renewed clarity of language and precision of doctrine the work of Dr. Bright and the prayers of Christians through the ages can have a wider use again.

I also must thank Eric Mathews of www.prayerandverse.com for proofreading the manuscript and for his helpful suggestions.

Commemoration of St. Augustine,
August 28, 2017.
Beaver Dam, Wisconsin, U. S. A.

Preface to the Original
Ancient Collects
by William Bright, D. D.

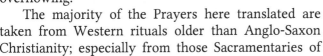

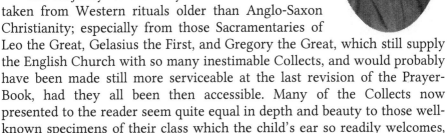

THE following pages are designed to contribute somewhat to a more practical knowledge among Churchmen of the devotional treasures to be found in ancient Service-books. They contain, it need not be said, the merest gatherings from an ample and splendid storehouse,—a few drops from a cup filled to overflowing.

The majority of the Prayers here translated are taken from Western rituals older than Anglo-Saxon Christianity; especially from those Sacramentaries of Leo the Great, Gelasius the First, and Gregory the Great, which still supply the English Church with so many inestimable Collects, and would probably have been made still more serviceable at the last revision of the Prayer-Book, had they all been then accessible. Many of the Collects now presented to the reader seem quite equal in depth and beauty to those well-known specimens of their class which the child's ear so readily welcomes, and the man's heart finds so inexhaustible.

Other Western Prayers have been admitted, of later date than the sixth century; and several Eastern ones, from the Liturgies of Jerusalem and Alexandria, popularly called after S. James and S. Mark, and traceable, in their "main order and substance," to the second century; from some other Liturgies historically connected with these, especially the great Liturgy of S. Chrysostom, the ordinary Rite of the Greek Church; and from the Daily Office and other Services of that Church.

The sources of the compilation are mainly these:—Muratori's Liturgia Romana Vetus; Menard's Liber Sacramentorum D. Gregorii; Pamelius' Liturgicon Latinum; Thomasius' Codices Sacrementorum; Mabillon De Liturgia Gallicana; Mr. G. H. Forbes's Gallican Liturgies; Martene De Antiquis Ecclesice Ritibus; the Mozarabic Missal and Breviary; the Ambrosian Missal; the Sarum Missal and Breviary; Maskell's Monumenta Ritualia; Goar's Euchologion; Benaudot's Liturgiarum Orientalium Collectio; the Missa Armenorum; and Neale's editions of Ancient Eastern Liturgies.

In regard to the translation, as little freedom as possible has been taken in the way of development or paraphrase. The often-recurring word *mereamur* has not been rendered "may deserve" or "may merit," because those verbs would convey a false notion of the original, making it express the doctrine of "condignity;" but by such words as "may obtain," or "may be enabled to have;" not by any means with a wish to ignore the fact, that it also sometimes implies the being "fitted" to obtain, and sometimes being "rewarded" with. This latter idea, when clearly distinguished from that of proper merit, we find in God's language both to Abraham and to the Apostles, and express in prayer during the week preceding Advent.

One section of the volume is devoted to Prayers for the exclusive use of the Clergy, with the Latin originals in most cases prefixed. But it is hoped that other passages will also prove helpful to pastors who, in the Visitation of the Sick, desire to follow the counsel of the late Professor Blunt in his admirable Lectures, and "treasure up any prayers they may meet with, such as ancient Liturgies and Sacramentaries,—a most pregnant mine,—or the devotions of worthies of the Church, may supply, which they may deem fitted for the sick chamber."

Some of the Collects or other prayers here presented may also be found available for the purposes of Family Prayer.

In the present Edition some inaccuracies have been corrected, and a considerable number of new prayers inserted, especially from the Leonine Sacramentary, and from the glowing and pathetic supplications of the ancient Spanish Church. In the arrangement of the prayers, also, some changes have been made with a view to greater facility in the use of the book. The "Prayers on the incarnation," as they were called in the first Edition, are now distributed according to the seasons of Advent, Christmas, Epiphany, Lent, Passion-tide, Easter, Ascension, Whitsuntide; and the "Prayers for particular Graces" are assigned to the Trinity season, in conformity to the general character of the Church Collects for that period. But as prayers of the latter class can never be inappropriate, so those of the former may, for the most part, be useful in carrying out, through the whole Christian year, the principle which would "teach and train men," as an accomplished writer on Liturgical subjects has expressed it," to base their prayer and to build up their life upon the Articles of the Creed." Most precious is that principle amid the darkening shadows of the great controversy between Faith and Unbelief — amid the deepening intensity of that heart-searching process which presents to each one of us the Person of Jesus Christ, our Master and only Saviour, very God and very Man, and propounds the question, "Will ye also go away?" If we would give the Apostle's answer, we must remember that our religion is one and indivisible; that to separate the morals from the mysteries, the practical element, as it is called, from the element of supernatural fact and of pure doctrine, is simply to destroy the whole fabric. The former, in truth, depends upon the latter; in the Creed of eighteen centuries "lies, we believe, the very pith and marrow of the Gospel." And if this be so, then surely the prayers of Christian people will be more accordant with the mind of Christ, and more instinct with a sense of the gloriousness of Christianity, in proportion as they dwell explicitly on "the great Mystery of Godliness," and appeal to the manifold graces laid up for us in the Mediatorial work of the God-Man.

It is in His hand, Whose are all the good words of His ancient servants, to cause them, however poorly rendered, to "bring forth more fruit in their age," and minister to the increase of a living faith in His incarnation among those for whom He died,—for whom He lives.[1]

University College, Oxford,
Whitsuntide, 1861.

PREFACE TO THE THIRD EDITION

IT would have been easy to enlarge this edition with additional matter, but that it seemed undesirable to increase the size of the book, and so render it less commodious as a Manual.

University College,
June 22, 1864.

---

[1] Bright's footnotes in his preface have been omitted since some of them were redundant with the text, and some referenced periodicals that are no longer available.

CONTENTS

INTRODUCTORY PRAYERS

Lord God,
Father of our Lord God and Savior Jesus Christ,
your name is great,
your nature is wonderful,
your goodness is inexhaustible,
you are God and Master of all things,
and are blessed forever.
You sit between the cherubim,
and are glorified by the seraphim.
Before you stand thousands of thousands
and ten thousand times ten thousand,
the hosts of holy angels and archangels.
Sanctify our souls and bodies and spirits,
calm our fears,
cleanse our consciences
and drive out every evil thought,
every selfish desire,
envy, pride, hypocrisy,
falsehood, deceit, anxiety,
covetousness, arrogance, laziness,
malice, anger, grudges,
blasphemy, deeds or thoughts
that are contrary to your holy will.
Lord, since you love us all,
give us the strength to boldly call on you
in the freedom of Christ, [1]
without condemnation,
with a pure heart and a contrite soul,
with undivided attention
and with sanctified lips,
as our holy God and Father in heaven. [1]

p. 1.1, Liturgy of St. James

Lord our God,
you are great, eternal, and wonderful in glory.
You keep your covenant and promises
for those who love you with all their heart.
You are the Life of all,
the Help of those who flee to you,
the Hope of those who cry to you.

---

[1] "in the freedom of Christ," added for clarity.

Cleanse us from our sins,
secret and open,
and from every thought that displeases you.
Cleanse our bodies and souls,
our hearts and consciences,
that with a pure heart and a clear soul,
with perfect love and calm hope,
we may come before you confidently
and fearlessly pray to you;
through Jesus Christ our Lord.[2] [2]

p. 2.1, Coptic Liturgy of St. Basil

O Lord,
show your favor to your people who pray to you,
that what we are moved to ask by your Word and Spirit,[3]
we may quickly receive by your goodness;
through Jesus Christ our Lord. [3]

p. 2.2, Leonine Sacramentary

O Lord, look on your servants who trust in you,
move us to ask for things that are pleasing to you,
and to receive your blessings with thanks;[4]
through Jesus Christ our Lord. [4]

p. 2.3, Leonine

O Lord our God,
you alone foresee and give us
what we need for our salvation.
Give us the desire to call to you,
and graciously give us what will be for our good;
through Jesus Christ our Lord. [5]

p. 2.4, Leonine

O Lord,
help us to persevere in prayer.
Do not forsake us in our troubles,
but protect us with your abundant grace
whenever we call to you;
through Jesus Christ our Lord. [6]

p. 3.1, Leonine

O Lord, mercifully hear the prayers of your people.
So that we may receive what we ask,

---

[2] "...through Jesus Christ our Lord" for doctrinal clarity and for a better ending.
[3] Original translation: "that what by Thy inspiration they faithfully ask," "they" was also changed to "we" in some prayers.
[4] Original translation: "...and also to obtain what they ask;"

2

always move us to ask for what pleases you;
through Jesus Christ our Lord. [7]

p. 3.2, Leonine, Trinity 10

O Lord,
govern the hearts of your faithful servants.
Purify our will,
and in your generosity,
give us your good things;
through Jesus Christ our Lord. [8]

p. 3.3, Leonine

O Lord,
make us obedient to you with a ready will,
and always stir up our wills to pray to you;
through Jesus Christ our Lord. [9]

p. 3.4, Gelasian Sacramentary

O Lord,
give your people devoted hearts.
Bring us together to seek your favor in our needs,
that we may willingly serve you as our King;
through Jesus Christ our Lord. [10]

p. 4.1, Gelasian

O God of hope,
you are the true light of the faithful,
the perfect brightness of the blessed,
and the true light of your Church.
Grant that our hearts may humbly pray to you
and always offer you our praise;
through Jesus Christ our Lord. [11]

p. 4.2, Gelasian

O Lord,
be with your faithful people.
Most loving God, as you move us to pray,
also give us comfort and help;
through Jesus Christ our Lord. [12]

p. 4.3, Gelasian

O God,
you are the life of the faithful
and the bliss of the righteous.
Hear the prayers of your people,
that those who thirst for your promises
may always be filled from your abundance;
through Jesus Christ our Lord. [13]

p. 4.4, Gelasian

DAILY MORNING PRAYERS

After the night our spirits awaken to you, O God,
for your Word is our light.
Teach us, O God, your righteousness,
your commandments, and your judgments.
Enlighten the eyes of our minds,
so that we do not sleep in the death of sin.
Drive away all darkness from our hearts.
Give us your Sun of Righteousness.
Guard our lives from all blame by the seal of your Holy Spirit.
Guide our steps into the way of peace.
Let us see the dawn and the day with joy,
that we may offer our prayers to you in the evening. [14]

p. 5.1, Daybreak Office of the Eastern Church

Lord God of our salvation,
we thank you
for all good things you do in our lives.
Help us always look to you,
the Savior and Benefactor of our souls.
You have refreshed us in the past night,
raised us up from our beds,
and brought us to worship your glorious name.
Give us grace and power
that we may sing your praise with understanding,
pray to you without ceasing,
and continue to work out our salvation
with fear and trembling;
through the aid of your Christ. [15]

p. 5.2, Daybreak Office of the Eastern Church

O loving Master,
shine into our hearts
by the pure light of knowing you,
open the eyes of our minds to reflect on your teaching,
and put into us the holy respect of your blessed commandments.
Lead us to set aside all that is worldly
that we may follow a spiritual life,
thinking and doing all things as it pleases you.
For you are our sanctification
and our illumination,
and to you we give all glory,
Father, Son, and Holy Spirit,
now and forever. [16]

p. 6.1, Daybreak Office of the Eastern Church

O God,
you divide the day from the night.
Give us hearts and minds
unshadowed by the gloom of evil,
that we may continually think about things
that are good and wholesome,
and always be pleasing in your sight;
through Jesus Christ our Lord.[5] [17]

p. 6.2, Gelasian

We give you thanks,
Holy Lord, Father almighty, eternal God,
for you have brought us through the night
to the hours of morning.
Grant that we may pass this day without sin,
that at evening we may again give you thanks;
through Jesus Christ our Lord. [18]

p. 6.3, Gelasian

O Lord,
hear the morning prayers of your people,
and enlighten our hearts with your healing goodness,
that no dark desires may trouble us,
since the light of your heavenly grace has renewed us;
through Jesus Christ our Lord. [19]

p. 7.1, Gelasian

O Lord,
shine your light into our hearts
that we may see the light of your commandments,
walk in your way and fall into no error;
through Jesus Christ our Lord. [20]

p. 7.2, Gelasian

Almighty and eternal God,
with you there is no darkness at all.
Shine your law into our hearts
that we may see the light of your commandments,
walk in your way and fall into no error;
through Jesus Christ our Lord.[6] [21]

p. 7.2, footnote, Gregorian

---

[5] This revision was influenced by other translations of the Latin prayer.
[6] [21] is based on Bright's comment in the footnote about the Gregorian variant of [20], and made to have a reference to 1 John 1:5.

O God, by the light of your Word
you scatter the darkness of ignorance.
Increase in our hearts
the power of faith you have given us,
that no temptations may put out the fire
your grace has caused to burn in our hearts;
through Jesus Christ our Lord. [22]

p. 7.3, Gelasian

O Lord,
pour the holy light of your love into our souls
that we may always be devoted to you.
By your wisdom we were created,
and by your providence we are governed;
through Jesus Christ our Lord. [23]

p. 7.4, Gelasian

O Lord,
let our prayers come before you in the morning.
You became fully human
and took on yourself our weakness and suffering.
Grant that we may pass this day in gladness and peace,
without stumbling and without stain,
that reaching the evening victorious over temptation,[7]
we may praise you as our eternal King;
through your mercy, O our God,
you are blessed,
and live and govern all things,
now and forever. [24]

p. 8.1, Mozarabic (Spanish)

---

[7] "...victorious over temptation" if from another translation/version of this prayer. Bright's translation had "...without any temptation,"

DAILY EVENING PRAYERS

In the evening and morning and noonday
we praise you, we thank you, and we pray:
Master of all,
let our prayers rise before you as incense.
Do not let our hearts turn away
to words or thoughts of wickedness,
but keep us from all things that might hurt us,
for our eyes look to you, O Lord,
and our hope is in you.
Do not let us be ashamed, O our God,
for the sake of Jesus Christ our Lord.[8] [25]

p. 9.1, Vespers of the Eastern Church

O Lord our God,
you opened the heavens,
and came down for the salvation of humanity.
Look on your servants and your inheritance,
for to you, an awesome and gracious Judge,
we bow in humble worship,
looking for no human help,
but waiting for your pardon and salvation.
Guard us at all times,
and protect us this evening
and in the coming night,
from every foe,
from every adverse working of the devil,
from idle thoughts and wicked plans. [26]

p. 9.2, Vespers of the Eastern Church

O Lord our God,
after the weariness of the day's labor,
refresh us with quiet sleep.
Give us the help we need in our weakness
that we may be devoted to you both in body and mind;
through Jesus Christ our Lord. [27]

p. 10.1, Leonine

---

[8] "...for the sake of Jesus Christ our Lord." added for doctrinal clarity and for a better ending.

O Lord,
hear our prayers,
and protect us by day and night,
that in all the changes of each day
we may always be strengthened
by your changelessness;
through Jesus Christ our Lord. [28]

p. 10.2, Leonine

Almighty and eternal God,
at evening, and morning, and noonday,
we humbly ask,
drive from our hearts the darkness of sin,
and lead us to the true Light
which is Christ;
through Jesus Christ our Lord. [29]

p. 10.3, Gelasian

Yours is the day, O Lord,
and yours is the night.
Let your Sun of Righteousness
remain in our hearts
to drive away the darkness
of wicked thoughts;
through Jesus Christ our Lord. [30]

p. 10.4, Gelasian

We give you thanks, O Lord,
because you have preserved us through the day.
We give you thanks
because you will preserve us through the night.
Bring us in safety, O Lord,
to the morning hours,
that you may receive our praise at all times;
through Jesus Christ, our Lord. [31]

p. 10.5, Gelasian

O God,
by making the evening to follow the day
you have given the gift of rest for human weakness.
Grant that as we enjoy your timely blessings,
we may acknowledge you
from whom they come. [32]

p. 11.1, Gelasian

O Lord God,
Life of mortals,
Light of the faithful,
strength of those who labor,
and the rest for your saints,
give us a peaceful night
free of all trouble,
that after quiet sleep
we may enjoy your blessings
at the return of the light,
and be empowered by your Holy Spirit,
and moved to give you thanks. [33]

p. 11.2, Mozarabic

FOR A SUNDAY OR HOLY-DAY MORNING

We give you thanks upon thanks,
O Lord our God,
Father of our Lord and Savior Jesus Christ,
by all means, at all times, in all places.
For you have sheltered, assisted,
supported, and led us on
through the past times of our lives,
and brought us to this hour.
O good and loving,
grant that we may pass this holy day,
and all the times of our lives, without sin,
with all joy, health, salvation,
sanctification, and fear of you.
O Lord God, drive away from us
and from your holy Christian[9] and apostolic Church
all envy, all fear, all temptation,
all the working of Satan,
and all conspiracy of wicked men.
Supply us with things good and profitable.
In whatever ways we have sinned against you,
in word, deed, or thought,
pass over in your love and goodness.
Do not forsake us, O God,
for we hope in you.
Lead us not into temptation,
but deliver us from the evil one
and from his works,
by the grace, compassion, and goodness
of your only Son. [34]

p. 12.1, from the Liturgy of St. Mark

The day of resurrection has dawned on us,
the day of true light and life,
in which Christ, the life of believers,
arose from the dead.
Let us give abundant thanks and praise to God,
that while we solemnly celebrate the day
of our Lord's resurrection,
he may bestow on us
quiet peace and special gladness,

---

[9] Original translation: "holy Catholic and Apostolic Church." Other uses of "Catholic" (meaning the universal Christian faith) have been changed to "Christian" when connected with the church.

10

so that being protected from morning to night
by his favoring mercy,
we may rejoice in the gift of our Redeemer. [35]

p. 13.1, Mozarabic

O Lord,
in this hour of this day
fill us with your mercy,
that we may rejoice throughout the whole day
and delight in your praise;
through Jesus Christ our Lord. [36]

p. 13.2, Sarum

FOR A SUNDAY OR HOLY-DAY EVENING

Blessed are you,
almighty Master,
for you have granted us to pass through this day,
and to reach the beginning of the night.
Hear our prayers,
and those of all your people,
and forgive us our voluntary and involuntary sins.
Accept our evening prayers,
and send down on your children
the fullness of your mercy and compassion.
Surround us with your holy angels.
Arm us with the armor of your righteousness.
Surround us with your truth.
Guard us with your power.
Deliver us from every assault and plan of the adversary,
and let us pass this evening and the coming night,
and all the days of our lives,
in fullness of peace and holiness,
without sin or stumbling.
For you pity and save,
O Christ our God. [37]

p. 14.1, Pentecost Vespers of the Eastern Church

O Lord,
grant that we may rejoice to see
the bliss of your Jerusalem,
and be carried there to constant gladness.
Since it is the home of the multitude of the saints,
through Christ may we also be counted worthy[10]
to have our portion there,
and that your only Son,
the Prince and Savior of all,
may in this world graciously relieve his afflicted,
and hereafter in his kingdom
be the eternal comfort of his redeemed. [38]

p. 14.1, Mozarabic

---

[10] "...through Christ may we..." was added for doctrinal clarity.

PRAYERS FOR SACRED SEASONS
ADVENT

O Lord,
stir up your power and come.
Mercifully fulfill all you have promised your Church
to the end of the world. [39]

p. 16.1, Gelasian

Stir up our hearts, O Lord,
to prepare the way for your only Son.
By his advent we may be enabled
to serve you with purified minds;
through Jesus Christ our Lord. [40]

p. 16.2, Gelasian

O Lord,
purify our consciences by your daily presence,
that when your Son, our Lord comes,
he may find in us a place prepared for himself;
through Jesus Christ our Lord. [41]

p. 16.3, Gelasian

O Lord our God,
make us watchful and heedful
as we await the coming of your Son,
Christ our Lord,
that when he comes and knocks
he will find us not sleeping in sins
but awake and rejoicing in his praises;
through Jesus Christ our Lord. [42]

p. 16.4, Gelasian

Almighty God,
let our souls be kindled by your Spirit,
that being filled by your divine gift
as lamps are filled with oil,
we may shine like blazing lights
before the presence
of your Son Christ when he comes again;
through the same Jesus Christ our Lord. [43]

p. 17.1, Gelasian

O Lord our God,
let us all rejoice with upright hearts,
gathered together in the unity of faith,
that at the coming of your Son our Savior,

we may meet him in the company of his saints;
through the same Jesus Christ our Lord. [44]

p. 17.2, Gelasian

Almighty God,
hear our prayers
and pour on us your loving tenderness,
that we who are afflicted by our sins
may be refreshed by the advent of our Savior;
through the same Jesus Christ our Lord. [45]

p. 17.3, Gelasian

O Lord our God,
clothe us with your divine power,
that at the coming
of our Lord Jesus Christ your Son,
we may be found worthy in him
of the banquet of eternal life;
through the same Jesus Christ our Lord. [46]

p. 17.4, Gelasian

Almighty God,
grant this grace to your people,
that we may be vigilant
for the coming of your only Son,
that as our Savior taught us,
we may prepare our souls
like blazing lamps to meet him;
through the same Jesus Christ our Lord. [47]

p. 18.1, Gelasian

O Lord,
incline your merciful ears to our prayers
and enlighten the darkness of our hearts
by the light of your visitation;
for you live and reign
with the Father and the Holy Spirit,
one God, now and forever. [48]

p. 18.2, Gelasian, Advent 3 until 1661

O Lord,
make us abhor our own evils
with all our heart,
that at the coming of your Son our Lord,
we may be ready to receive his good things;
through the same Jesus Christ our Lord. [49]

p. 18.3, Gelasian

O Lord,
mercifully hear the prayers of your people.
Just as we rejoice in the advent
of your only Son in the flesh,
when he comes a second time in his majesty
we will receive his reward of eternal life;
through the same Jesus Christ our Lord. [50]

p. 18.4, Gelasian

Almighty God,
grant that the coming celebration
of our redemption
may both help us in this present life,
and enrich us with the bliss of life eternal;
through Jesus Christ our Lord. [51]

p. 19.1, Gelasian

O Lord,
be our crown of glory
when you come to judge the world by fire.
Clothe us here
with the robe of your righteousness,
and hereafter with the perfection
of glorious liberty;
through your mercy, O our God,
you are blessed,
and live and govern all things,
now and forever. [52]

p. 19.2, Mozarabic

Come to deliver us,
O Lord God of hosts.
Turn us again,
and show your face,
and we will be saved.
Being cleansed by your mercy
with the gift of repentance,
we may stand before you in the judgment;
through your mercy, O our God,
you are blessed,
and live and govern all things,
now and forever. [53]

p. 19.3, Mozarabic

O Christ our God,
you will come to judge the world
in the humanity you have taken on yourself.
Sanctify us wholly,
that in the day of your coming
our whole spirit, soul, and body
may arise to a fresh life in you,
that we may live and reign with you forever. [54]

p. 19.4, Mozarabic

Lord God, Father almighty,
purify the secrets of our hearts,
and mercifully wash out all the stains of sin.
O Lord, cleanse us from our crimes
by your tender blessing,
that we may await without any terror
the fearful and terrible coming
of Jesus Christ our Lord. [55]

p. 19.5, Mozarabic

O God,
you looked on man
when he had fallen into death,
and resolved to redeem him
by the advent of your only Son.
Grant that those who confess
his glorious incarnation
may also be received
to the fellowship of him, their Redeemer;
through the same Jesus Christ our Lord. [56]

p. 20.1, Gallican (Central Gaul)

O Wisdom,
coming forth from the mouth of the Most High,
reaching from one end to the other,
mightily and sweetly ordering all things;
Come and teach us the way of understanding. [57]

p. 20.2a, Sarum

O *Adonai*,
and leader of the house of Israel,
who appeared to Moses in the fire of the burning bush
and gave him the law on Sinai;
Come and redeem us with an outstretched arm. [58]

p. 20.2b, Sarum

O Root of Jesse,
standing as a sign among the peoples;
before you kings will shut their mouths,

16

to you the nations will make their prayer;
Come and deliver us, and delay no longer. [59]

p. 20.2c, Sarum

O Key of David
and Scepter of the house of Israel,
what you open no one can shut.
What you shut no one can open.
Come and lead the prisoners from the prison house,
who dwell in darkness and the shadow of death. [60]

p. 20.2d, Sarum

O Morning Star,
splendor of light eternal
and Sun of righteousness;
Come and enlighten
those who dwell in darkness and the shadow of death. [61]

p. 20.2e, Sarum

O King of the nations,
and their desire,
the cornerstone making both one;
Come and save the human race,
which you fashioned from clay. [62]

p. 20.2f, Sarum

O Emmanuel,
our King and our Lawgiver,
the hope of the nations and their Savior;
Come and save us, O Lord our God. [63]

p. 20.2g, Sarum

CHRISTMAS

O God,
you gladden us
with the yearly anticipation of our redemption.
Grant that we who now joyfully receive
your only Son as our Redeemer
may also see him without fear
when he comes as our judge;
our Lord Jesus Christ,
who with you and the Holy Spirit
lives and reigns,
one God, now and forever. [64]

p. 21.1, Gelasian, Christmas Day I

O merciful God,
grant that our minds may be prepared
for the reception of the wonder
of your Son's nativity,
and the hearts of unbelievers be subdued;
through the same Jesus Christ our Lord. [65]

p. 21.2, Gelasian

O God,
you have made this holy night shine
with the brightness of the true Light.
Grant that we who have known
the mysteries of that Light here on earth
may come to the fullness
of his joys in heaven;
through the same Jesus Christ our Lord. [66]

p. 22.1, Gelasian

(The above Collects may be said on Christmas Eve.)
Merciful God,
grant that he who was born this day
to be the Savior of the world,
since he is the Author of our divine birth,
may also bestow on us immortality;
through the same Jesus Christ our Lord. [67]

p. 22.2, Leonine

Almighty and eternal God,
you willed that the beginning and end of all religion
should depend on the nativity
of our Lord Jesus Christ, your Son.
May we also be counted as members of his body,
on whom is built the whole salvation of humanity;
with you and the Holy Spirit
he lives and reigns,
one God, now and forever. [68]

p. 22.3, Leonine

O Lord,
bestow on your servants
the increase of faith, hope, and love,
that as we glory in the nativity of your Son, our Lord,
we may, by your governance,
not feel the adversities of this world,
and that what we desire to celebrate in time,
we may also enjoy to all eternity;
through the same Jesus Christ our Lord. [69]

p. 22.4, Leonine

O God,
you were pleased to save the human race
which was mortally wounded by the fall of Adam,
by the nativity of your Christ.
Grant that we may not follow our ancestor in sin,
but be transferred to the fellowship of our Redeemer;
who lives and reigns
with you and the Holy Spirit,
one God, now and forever. [70]

p. 23.1, Leonine

O Lord our God,
grant that we who rejoice to keep the feast
of the nativity of Jesus Christ our Lord
may walk with him
and receive fellowship with him;
through the same Jesus Christ our Lord. [71]

p. 23.2, Leonine

O Lord,
strengthen the faith of your people,
that as we confess the birth
of your glorious and eternal Son in human flesh,
born of his virgin mother,
we may be delivered from all earthly troubles,
and receive your eternal joys;
through the same Jesus Christ our Lord. [72]

p. 23.3, Leonine. Bright comments that this and the following prayer
emphasize Christ as one person but with two natures, rejecting
ancient Nestorian and Eutychian heresies

O Lord our God,
grant that your Church may understand
both parts of the one mystery,
and adore one Christ,
true God and fully human,
not divided from our nature
nor separate from your essence;
through the same Jesus Christ our Lord. [73]

p. 23.4, Leonine

Almighty God,
grant that the new birth
of your only Son in the flesh
may set us free
from the old bondage
under the yoke of sin;
through the same Jesus Christ our Lord. [74]

p. 24.1, Leonine

O our God,
grant that your family,
which has been saved
by the nativity of your Son,
our Lord Jesus Christ,
may also find our rest in him,
our eternal Redeemer;
who lives and reigns
with you and the Holy Spirit,
one God, now and forever. [75]

p. 24.2, Gelasian

Almighty and eternal God,
by your only Son
you have made us your new creation.
Preserve the works of your mercy,
and cleanse us from all our ancient stains,
that by your grace
we may become like him
who dwells with you, still fully human;
through the same Jesus Christ our Lord. [76]

p. 24.3, Gelasian

O Lord,
hear our prayers,
and let your people
whom you have made and restored,
also be saved by your unending work;
through Jesus Christ our Lord. [77]

p. 24.4, Gelasian

Almighty God,
as the new light of your incarnate Word
enlightens our minds by faith,
may it also shine forth in our actions;
through the same Jesus Christ our Lord. [78]

p. 25.1, Gregorian

Almighty God,
with a wondrous, new and heavenly light,
our Savior went forth to redeem the world.
May his salvation also shine forth
in the renewal of our hearts;
through the same Jesus Christ our Lord. [79]

p. 25.2, Gregorian

Merciful and most loving God,
by your will and mercy
Jesus Christ our Lord
humbled himself to exalt all humanity,
and descended to the depths to lift up the lowly,
and was born of a virgin, fully God and fully human,
to restore in us your holy image that had been lost.
Grant that your people may cling to you,
that as you have redeemed us in your mercy,
we may always please you by devoted service. [80]

p. 25.3, Gallican

Blessed be the Lord God,
who comes in the name of the Lord,
and has dawned on us.
His coming has redeemed us,
his nativity has enlightened us,
and by his coming has found the lost
and shined on those who sat in darkness.
Grant, O Father almighty,
that we who celebrate the day of his birth
may find the day of judgment a day of mercy.
And as we have known his goodness as our Redeemer,
we may feel his gentle tenderness as our Judge. [81]

p. 26.1, Mozarabic

We give you thanks,
O Lord our God,
and bless you from day to day
for bringing us to this, your holy celebration.
May we, with all your faithful people,
welcome this your birthday
in peace and quietness through many succeeding years;
through your mercy, O our God,
you are blessed,
and live and govern all things,
now and forever. [82]

p. 26.2, Mozarabic

Almighty and eternal God,
you have hallowed this day
by the incarnation of your Word,
and his birth of the virgin Mary.
As your people share in this celebration,
may we who have been redeemed by your grace
be happy as your adopted children;
through the same Jesus Christ our Lord. [83]

p. 26.3, Gelasian / Gregorian

21

Almighty and eternal God,
you are the light of the faithful
and the ruler of souls,
and you have hallowed us
by the incarnation of your Word,
and by his birth of the virgin Mary.
Let the power of your Holy Spirit come also on us,
and the mercy of the most high overshadow us. [84]

p. 27.1, Mozarabic

O Christ,
almighty Son of God,
come graciously on the day of your nativity
to be the Savior of your people,
that with your goodness
you may deliver us from all anxiety
and all temporal fear;
you live and reign with the Father and the Holy Spirit,
one God, now and forever. [85]

p. 27.2, Ambrosian

O Lord,
enlighten our hearts
by the holy radiance of your Son's incarnation.
In him, may we escape the darkness of this world,
and by his guidance reach the country of eternal brightness;
through the same Jesus Christ our Lord. [86]

p. 27.3, Sarum / Gelasian

O God,
you have made the most glorious name
of your only Son, our Lord Jesus Christ,
very sweet and supremely lovable
to your faithful servants,
and fearful and terrible to those who hate you.
Grant that all
who devoutly venerate this name of Jesus on earth
may in this life receive the sweetness of holy comfort,
and in the life to come receive the joy of exulting gladness
and never-ending joy;
through the same Jesus Christ our Lord. [87]

p. 27.4, Sarum Missal

EPIPHANY

O God,
your only Son
appeared in substance of our flesh.

Grant that through him
who became like us in every way,
we may receive an inward renewal;
through the same Jesus Christ our Lord. [88]

p. 28.1, Gelasian

Almighty and eternal God,
you made known the incarnation of your Word
by the testimony of a glorious star.
When the wise men saw it,
they adored your majesty with gifts.
Let the star of your righteousness
always shine in our hearts,
and our treasure consist
in giving thanks to you;
through Jesus Christ our Lord. [89]

p. 28.2, Gelasian

O God,
you enlighten all nations.
Give your people the constant joy of peace,
and pour into our hearts
that radiant light
you shined into the minds
of the wise men;
through Jesus Christ our Lord. [90]

p. 28.3, Gelasian

O Lord,
enlighten your people,
and always set our hearts on fire
with the brightness of your glory,
that we may always acknowledge our Savior,
and truly receive our Lord;
who lives and reigns with you and the Holy Spirit,
one God, now and forever. [91]

p. 28.4, Gelasian

Almighty and eternal God,
you are the brightness of the faithful.
You have made this day holy
by the first-fruits of the chosen Gentiles.
Fill the world with your glory
and show yourself by the radiance of your light
to the nations that are subject to you;
through Jesus Christ our Lord. [92]

p. 29.1, Gregorian

O Lord,
mercifully correct our wanderings
and by your compassion
guide us to the saving vision of your truth;
through Jesus Christ our Lord. [93]

p. 29.2, Gregorian

O God,
through your only Son Jesus Christ our Lord
you blessed the regenerating waters with the grace
which sanctifies us for eternal salvation.
You yourself descended on him with your Spirit
as a mysterious dove on his head.
Give your whole Church a blessing
that always keeps us safe,
blesses all your servants,
directs the course of those who follow you,
and opens the door of your heavenly kingdom
to all who are waiting to enter;
through Jesus Christ our Lord. [94]

p. 29.3, Gothic (Southern Gaul)

O glorious, holy, almighty God,
you always pity the many wanderings of humanity,
and for this reason, you guided the Magi,
who lived in a land of dark superstition,
to your sacred cradle by the light of a star,
that you might enlighten all
who were walking in their own errors
with the desire of knowing you.
Enlighten us also with burning love for you,
that we who already know you
by your gracious illumination,
may cling to you forever. [95]

p. 30.1, Mozarabic

O almighty God,
grant that we may be able
to always shake off the yoke
of the slavery of sin,[11]
and to appear before your majesty
in our heavenly country;
through Jesus Christ our Lord. [96]

p. 30.2, Ambrosian

---

[11] Original translation: "of Egyptian servitude and sin,..."

24

LENT, OR OTHER FAST-DAYS

O Lord,
grant that we may enter
this sacred season
with fitting piety,
and go through it
with undisturbed devotion;
through Jesus Christ our Lord. [97]

p. 30.3, Gregorian

Lord,
grant that may enter
the service of our Christian warfare
with our eyes on you,
that as we fight against the spiritual powers of wickedness
we may be strengthened by your victory;
through Jesus Christ our Lord.[12] [98]

p. 31.1, Leonine

O God,
by your Word
you marvelously worked out
the reconciliation of humanity.
During this holy fast
may we devote ourselves to you with all our hearts,
and be united with each other in prayer to you;
through Jesus Christ our Lord. [99]

p. 31.2, Gelasian

O God,
in your deep counsel
and foresight for humanity,
you sent your Son to heal the hearts of the weak[13]
and purify our souls and bodies.
You are the Savior of body and soul.
You are the loving bestower of eternal happiness!
Jesus Christ our Lord. [100]

p. 31.3, Gelasian

---

[12] Original translation: "...warfare with holy fasting; that as we fight against the spiritual powers of wickedness, we may be fortified by the aid of self-denial".

[13] "sent your Son..." Original translation: "...hast appointed holy fasts, whereby the hearts of the weak might receive salutary healing..."

O Lord,
let your gracious favor
carry us through the fast we have begun,
that as we observe it by bodily discipline
we may complete it with sincerity of mind;
through Jesus Christ our Lord. [101]

p. 31.4, Gelasian

Almighty God,
grant that by the annual exercise
of Lenten observances
we may grow in our knowledge
of the mystery of Christ,
and follow his mind
by conduct worthy of our calling;
through the same Jesus Christ our Lord. [102]

p. 31.5, Gelasian

O Lord,
sanctify our hearts,
and mercifully grant us
forgiveness of all our sins;
through Jesus Christ our Lord. [103]

p. 32.1, Gelasian

O Lord,
help us by your grace
that we may focus
on fasting and prayer, [14]
and be delivered from bodily and spiritual enemies;
through Jesus Christ our Lord. [104]

p. 32.2, Gelasian

Lord, eternal King of all,
grant that being purified by the sacred fast,
we may come with sincere minds
to partake of your holy things;
through Jesus Christ our Lord. [105]

p. 32.3, Gelasian

O Lord,
grant that renewing our sacred observances
with annual devotion,
we may please you both in body and soul;
through Jesus Christ our Lord. [106]

p. 32.4, Gelasian

---

[14] Alternate reading: "...on your Word and prayer,"

Lord,
let our earnest devotion
become fruitful through your grace,
for then will our fast be profitable to us
if it pleases your loving-kindness;
through Jesus Christ our Lord. [107]

p. 32.5, Gelasian

O Lord,
give our fasting a good effect,
that the mortification of our flesh
makes us focus on nourishment for our souls;
through Jesus Christ our Lord. [108]

p. 33.1, Gelasian

O God,
you spared the people of Nineveh
when they repented of their sins. [15]
In your mercy,
grant us also your forgiveness;
through Jesus Christ our Lord. [109]

p. 33.2, Old Gallican

Several of the penitential collects may be found suitable for ordinary use.

O God,
if you would give us what we deserve,
we would quickly perish.
Mercifully forgive our wanderings
and abide with us with your great mercy
that we may be inclined
to keep your commandments;
through Jesus Christ our Lord. [110]

p. 33.3, Leonine

O Lord,
in your forgiving love,
turn away what we deserve for our sins,
and do not let our offences prevail before you
but let your mercy always rise up to overcome them;
through Jesus Christ our Lord. [111]

p. 33.4, Leonine

O God,
you do not desire the death of sinners,
but that they turn from their ways and live.
Do not repay us with what we deserve for our sins,

---

[15] Original translation: "when they fasted for their sins."

27

and in your mercy, keep us from returning to sin
so that we do not fall under your judgment,
but help us amend our lives and enjoy your pardon;
through Jesus Christ our Lord. [112]

p. 33.5, Leonine

O Lord,
hear our prayer.
Do not let your mercy be far from your servants.
Heal our wounds, forgive our sins,
and let no sin separate us from you,
that we may always cling to you, our Lord. [113]

p. 34.1, Leonine

You brought the lost sheep home to the fold on your shoulders,
you received the prayers and confession of the tax collector.
O Lord, show your favor also to your servants.
Graciously receive our prayers. [114]

p. 34.2, Gelasian

O Lord,
let your mercy surround your servants,
and all our sins be blotted out by your pardon;
through Jesus Christ our Lord. [115]

p. 34.3, Gelasian

O God,
most gracious maker
and most merciful restorer of humanity.
When Adam and Eve were tempted by the devil and lost eternal life,
you redeemed humanity with the blood of your only Son.
Give life to your servants,
whose death you do not desire.
You do not forsake your people when they go astray,
but receive them when they return.
In your pity, hear the cries of your servants.
Heal their wounds.
Save those who turn to you.
Do not let your Church lose any member of her body,
so that those who were born again in baptism
will not be possessed by the second death.
Spare those who confess their sins,
that moved by you, they may mourn over their sins
and in the day of the dreadful judgment
escape the sentence of eternal damnation,
and know neither the terrors of the darkness
nor the fury of the flame.
Having returned from error

to the path of righteousness,
they may be pierced with no more wounds,
but may retain what your grace has given
and what your mercy has restored
in fullness forever;
through the same our Lord Jesus Christ. [116]

p. 35.1, Gelasian / Gregorian

O God,
beneath your eyes every heart trembles
and all consciences are afraid.
Be merciful to the groanings of all
and heal their wounds.
Since none of us is free from fault,
do not shut out any from your pardon;
through Jesus Christ our Lord. [117]

p. 36.1, Gelasian

Almighty and merciful God,
you do not desire the death of sinners,
only their faults.
Restrain the anger we deserve,
and pour out on us the kindness we ask,
that through your mercy
we may pass from mourning into joy;
through Jesus Christ our Lord. [118]

p. 36.2, Gelasian

O Lord,
in your kindness
show us your inexpressible mercy.
Set us free from our sins,
and rescue us from the punishment
we deserve for our sins;
through Jesus Christ our Lord. [119]

p. 36.3, Gelasian / Sarum

O God,
you purify the hearts
of those who confess their sins to you,
and you absolve accusing consciences
from all bonds of guilt.
Pardon the guilty
and give healing to the wounded
that they may receive forgiveness of all sins

and persevere in sincere devotion,
and not lose eternal redemption;
through Jesus Christ our Lord. [120]

p. 36.4, Gelasian

O God the Trinity,
your name is wonderful.
You purify the depths of the heart from vices
and make it whiter than the snow.
Give us your compassion.
Renew our hearts by your Holy Spirit
so that we may declare your praise.
Strengthen us by your righteous and royal Spirit
and give us a place in the heavenly Jerusalem;
through Jesus Christ our Lord. [121]

p. 37.1, Gallican

Before your eyes, O Lord,
I stand guilty by the witness of my own conscience.
I hardly dare to ask for what I do not deserve.
For you, Lord, know what we do.
We blush to confess what we do not fear to commit.
I return to you after falling into sin.
After wandering, I lie before you sorely wounded.
I am worthless.
My only relief is in you, good Physician!
Everywhere you find us.
To you alone we flee.
From you we cannot escape.
Let your forgiveness comfort those terrified by guilt.
We plead guilty before you, Lord.
Spare us, because you are kind.
We know that if you did not pardon
you would justly punish us.
But with you is great mercy
and overflowing readiness to forgive.
Your loving-kindness is our hope.
Do not give us what we deserve for our sins,
but hear our prayer. [122]

p. 37.2, From various "Apologiae Sacerdotis" in Menard's Gregorian Sacramentary

O God,
you do not desire the death of the wicked,
but that sinners come to repentance.
We are wretched and frail sinners.
Do not reject us from your tender love
or look on our sins and crimes

or our unclean and base thoughts
that set us apart from your will,
but look to your own mercy. [123]

p. 38.1, Gregorian / Menard

Receive my confession,
my only hope of salvation,
Jesus Christ, my Lord and God.
For in (*the penitent person may confess specific sins*) I am lost,
and altogether in thought, word, and deed,
and in all evils, I am overwhelmed.
You justify the ungodly and quicken the dead.
Lord my God, justify me and revive me.
Save me, O Lord, King of eternal glory.
Grant me to will and to do
what is pleasing to you and profitable for myself.
Give me help me in distress,
consolation in persecution,
and strength in all temptation.
Give me pardon for past evils,
amendment of present evils,
and protect me against evils to come.
You move us to sorrow for our sins.
I weep for my sins.
Erase them speedily, like a cloud.
O Lord, forget my sins, and remember your mercies.
O Christ, spare and pity me,
not as I deserve, but according to your mercy.
Do not despise me, a sinner.
Do not cast me away,
but receive me as you have promised, that I may live.
Give me a fountain of tears, Fountain of life.
My hope of salvation is in no works of mine,
but my soul hangs simply on the boundlessness of your love,
and confides in the greatness of your mercy. [124]

p. 38.2, Missal of Matthias Flaccus Illyricus, 1557

Almighty and eternal God,
you call into being things that are not,
and with you, what is hidden becomes visible.
Cleanse foolishness from our heart,
and purify us from our secret vices,
that we may to serve you, O Lord,
with a pure mind;
through Jesus Christ our Lord. [125]

p. 39.2, Gelasian

Hear our prayer, O Lord,
and listen to our groaning,
for we acknowledge our iniquities,
and lay open our sins before you.
Against you, O God, have we sinned.
To you we make our confession
and ask forgiveness.
Turn your face again, Lord,
to your servants you redeemed
with your own blood.
Spare us,
pardon our sins,
and extend to us your loving-kindness
and your mercy. [126]

p. 40.1, Mozarabic

O good Jesus,
you called Lazarus
to rise from the tomb.
May we hear your voice in our souls
and rise by grace from the depths of our own sin. [127]

p. 40.2, Mozarabic

O Lord,
cleanse our consciences
by the sincere confession of the Christian faith,
and by continual contrition of heart,
that we may always be heard by you in heaven
when we call to you for pardon for our sins on earth. [128]

p. 40.3, Mozarabic

O Lord,
let your forgiveness come from above.
May it comfort us in our misery,
may it cleanse us from our offences,
may it be granted to the penitent,
may it plead for mourners,
may it bring back those who wander from the faith,
may it raise up those who are fallen into sins,
may it reconcile us to the Father,
may it confirm us with the grace of Christ,
may it conform us to the Holy Spirit. [129]

p. 40.4. Mozarabic, Good Friday Litany

PASSIONTIDE

It is truly good and right
that we should give you thanks, Lord God,
through Jesus Christ your Son,
who, being God eternal,
was pleased to become fully human for our salvation.
O single, unequaled mystery of our Savior!
For he, being one and the same,
God most high, and perfect Man,
is both supreme High Priest and most sacred sacrifice.
In his divine power he created all things,
and in his human condition he delivered humanity.
By the power of his sacrifice he atoned for those stained by sin,
in right of his priesthood he reconciled those alienated from God.
O single, unequaled mystery of redemption
by which those ancient wounds
were healed by the Lord's new medicine,
and the judgment passed before on the first man
was lifted by the gifts of our Savior.
In self-indulgence Adam reached his hands to the tree.
In loving patience Christ fixed his hands to the cross.
Therefore the punishment borne by innocence
became the freedom of the debtor,
for debts are remitted to debtors
paid by him who owed nothing. [130]

p. 41.1, Old Gallican

Almighty and eternal God,
you have restored us
by the blessed Passion of your Christ.
Preserve in us the work of your mercy,
that by the celebration of this mystery
our lives may be continually devout;
through the same Jesus Christ our Lord [131]

p. 42.1, Leonine

O Lord,
purify your family,
and cleanse it from all corruption of evil,
that those who have been redeemed
by their Lord's Passion
may never again be stained
by the unclean spirit,
but may be possessed by eternal salvation;
through the same Jesus Christ our Lord. [132]

p. 42.2, Leonine

Remember your great mercy and love, O Lord,
and sanctify and protect your servants
whom Christ your Son redeemed by his blood;[16]
through the same Jesus Christ our Lord. [133]

p. 42.3, Gelasian

O God,
by the Passion of Christ our Lord
you destroyed the inherited death
from that ancient sin
that came to all Adam's children.
Just as we have borne
the image of the earthly Adam by our birth,
we may also be made holy by your grace
and bear the image of the heavenly Christ;
who lives and reigns with you and the Holy Spirit,
one God, now and forever. [134]

p. 42.4, Gelasian

Almighty God,
grant that we
who have failed in our weakness
through so many troubles
may be relieved by the intervention
of the Passion of your only Son;
through the same Jesus Christ our Lord. [135]

p. 43.1, Gregorian

Almighty God,
grant that we
who are always afflicted
by our own transgressions,
may be delivered by the Passion
of your only Son;
who lives and reigns with you and the Holy Spirit,
one God, now and forever. [136]

p. 43.2, Gregorian

O God,
for us you sent
your only Son
to endure the torture of the cross
and defeat the power of the enemy.

---

16 Original translation: "for whom Christ Thy Son by His Blood appointed unto us the Paschal mystery;"

Grant that we, your servants,
receive the grace of resurrection;
through the same Jesus Christ our Lord. [137]

p. 43.3, Gregorian

O loving Wisdom of the living God,
living Word and Power of God the eternal Father,
your birth is from of old, from ancient days,
Son of God the eternal Father.
You are God,
without whom nothing is,
by whom all things were created.
You are God above us,
and you became fully human for our sakes.
You have willed us to be what we are.
Give us what you have promised to all,
that your passion may be our deliverance,
and your death our life,
and your cross our redemption,
and your wounds our healing,
that being crucified with you,
we may be lifted up on high to your Father by your gift,
with whom you live and reign in bliss with the Holy Spirit,
one God, now and forever. [138]

p. 43.4, Old Gallican

O God,
for our redemption
you received the blood of Jesus Christ.
Destroy the works of the devil
and break through all the snares of sin,
that those who have been created by a new birth
may not be defiled by the old corruption. [139]

p. 44.1, Gothic

Lord Jesus Christ,
you stretched out your hands on the cross
and you redeemed us by your blood.
Forgive me, a sinner,
for none of my thoughts are hidden from you.
Pardon I ask,
pardon I hope for,
pardon I trust I have.
You are compassionate and merciful.
Spare and forgive me. [140]

p. 44.2, Ambrosian

Lord Jesus Christ, Son of the living God,
for our redemption
you were born and circumcised,
rejected by the Jews,
betrayed with a kiss by Judas,
seized, bound, and led in chains
to Annas, Caiaphas, Herod, and Pilate,
and you stood before them to be mocked,
smitten with palm and fist,
with the scourge and rod.
Your face was defiled with spitting.
You were crowned with thorns
and accused by false witnesses.
You were condemned,
and as an innocent Lamb led to slaughter,
bearing your own cross,
pierced with nails.
You were given gall and vinegar to drink
and you were left on the cross
to die the most shameful of deaths,
and then wounded with a spear.
By these your most sacred pains
you deliver us from all sins and penalties.
By your holy cross
bring us poor sinners
where you brought the repentant thief;
for you live and with the Father and the Holy Spirit,
one God, now and forever. [141]

p. 45.3, Sarum Missal, Innocent III

Gracious Lord almighty,
Jesus Christ,
let your sufferings aid us,
and defend us from all pain and grief,
all peril and misery,
all uncleanness of heart,
all sin, all scandal and infamy,
from evil diseases of soul and body,
from sudden and unforeseen death,
and from all persecution of our foes visible and invisible.
We know that whenever we remember your Passion,
we will find our safety in you.
Relying on your infinite tenderness,
most loving Savior,
protect and help us
and preserve us from all evil

by your most blessed and sacred sufferings
and continual tender love. [142]

p. 45.1, Sarum Missal

O God,
Son of God,
so loving, yet hated,
so patient, yet assaulted and killed,
you showed yourself gentle and merciful
even to your persecutors.
You have atoned for our sins
through the wounds of your Passion.
As you humbled yourself and suffered death for us,
now, in your glory,
shine on us with your eternal brightness. [143]

p. 46.1, Mozarabic

O Christ,
Son of God,
whom the crowd persecuted with blind fury,
and while they inflicted suffering on you as Man
because they did recognize the essence of your Divinity,
grant that we who confess you,
true God and Man, to be One Christ,
may be removed far away from eternal punishment. [144]

p. 46.2, Mozarabic

Jesus, our God,
you gave your cheek to those who struck you,
and for our sakes you endured mockery.
Teach us by the example of your Passion
to take your easy yoke and your light burden
and learn from you, since you are gentle and lowly in heart [145]

p. 46.3, Mozarabic

O Christ,
Son of God,
your Father gave you up for us all
when he received you as a true sacrifice for us.
Receive the prayers of your people.
Save those you have redeemed.
Give life to those you have delivered.
Do not let those you redeemed perish eternally.
Since you were crucified for all,
give us forgiveness of sins in this life,
and eternal joy in the life to come. [146]

p. 47.1, Mozarabic

Remember, O Jesus,
the vinegar and gall,
that bitter cup you tasted for the ungodly,
and let the bitterness you endured
be our unending sweetness. [147]

p. 47.2, Mozarabic

Lord Jesus Christ,
Son of the living God,
you came down from heaven to earth
from your Father's side,
suffered five wounds on the wood of the cross,
and shed your precious blood
for the forgiveness of our sins.
At the day of judgment
set us at your right hand.
Speak to us those sweet words,
"Come, you who are blessed by my Father,
inherit the kingdom prepared for you;"
with the Father and the Holy Spirit
you live and reign,
one God,
now and forever. [148]

p. 47.3, Sarum Missal

Lord Jesus Christ,
you went to the wood of the cross
for the redemption of the world
to enlighten the whole world
which was in deep darkness.
Shine your light into our souls and bodies
that we may receive your light eternal;
with the Father and the Holy Spirit
you live and reign,
one God,
now and forever. [149]

p. 48.1, Sarum Missal

By the shedding of the blood of Christ our Lord,
peace has been established in heaven and earth.
Truly precious is the covenant of peace
made by the offering of that holy blood!
Not with gold or silver,
not with gems or pearls,
but with the blood that poured

from the side of the Savior,
which gladdened heaven,
purified earth,
and terrified hell. [150]

p. 48.2, Gallican Sacramentary

The following five prayers are specifically for Good Friday.

Today, O good Jesus,
you did not hide your face from shame and spitting for us.
Today, Jesus our Redeemer,
you were mocked,
struck by unbelievers,
and crowned with thorns for us.
Today, good Shepherd,
you laid down your life for the sheep on the cross,
and you were crucified with robbers,
and had your sacred hands nailed through.
Today you were laid in the guarded tomb,
and the saints burst open their tombs.
Today, good Jesus,
you put an end to our sins,
that on the day of your resurrection
we may joyfully receive your holy body,
and be refreshed with your sacred blood. [151]

p. 48.3, Mozarabic

O Christ,
only Son of the eternal Father,
for us you were slain this day,
the Innocent for the ungodly.
Remember the price of your blood,
and blot out the sins of all your people.
As you patiently endured reproaches,
spitting, bonds, blows, scourge,
cross, nails, the bitter cup,
death, spear, and burial for us,
give us the infinite blessedness
of your heavenly kingdom.
As we bow down in reverence for your Passion,
lift us up with the heavenly joys of your resurrection. [152]

p. 49.1, Mozarabic

O Christ, God, great *Adonai,*
crucify us with yourself to this world,
that your life may be in us.
Take our sins on yourself to crucify them.

Draw us also to yourself,
since you were lifted up from the earth
to deliver us from the devil.
In the flesh and in sins we are under the devil's power,
yet we want to serve you, not him.
We desire to live under your authority,
and beg to be governed by you.
You endured the death of the cross
to deliver us mortals.
For this we worship you
and today we humbly adore,
implore, and invoke you,
O God, eternal Might,
come to us.
By your power you make things future
to be as things past,
and things past
to be as things present.
Your Passion is as saving to us
as if it happened today;
you live and reign
with the Father and the Holy Spirit.
Reign over us, Man, God,
Christ Jesus, King forever and ever. [153]

p. 49.2, prayer for noonday on Good Friday, Old Gallican

Jesus Christ, our Lord and God,
help us cling to you,
for you have delivered us from evil
and established us continually in good.
Break in pieces all the snares of our enemy.
Accept our devotion and hear our prayer,
now, and at all times.
Grant us peace and quietness,
piety, pure love, and grace
by the wounds of your Passion;
our God, Son of God,
you live with God the Father and reign with the Holy Spirit,
one God in Trinity,
abiding through all ages. [154]

p. 50.1, Mozarabic

Speak to our hearts,
Christ our Overseer,
and say to us,
"Be strong and take heart."
You helped and strengthened your people of old.

40

You will do the same now, for you are almighty.
O most loving Lord,
you will do what we cannot imagine,
for nothing is impossible to you, almighty God!
Truly, O Savior,
for us your body was red with blood.
You "washed your garment in wine,
and your clothes in the blood of grapes,"
for you are God alone, crucified for us,
whom the old transgression gave over to death.
By your wounds,
the countless wounds of our sins
have been healed.
O loving and crucified Christ, redeem us.
Save us, O loving Goodness;
O God, who reigns with the Father and the Holy Spirit,
one God forever, throughout all ages. [155]

p. 50.2, Old Gallican

EASTER

Hear us,
O Lord, Father almighty,
through Jesus Christ, the second Adam,
that being buried with Jesus your Son,
and raised up again by his life,
we may receive forgiveness through him
in this night of his holy resurrection,
by the grace that attends this celebration,
by his gift and your blessing,
and the counsel and mysterious working of the Holy Spirit;
who lives and reigns with you,
one God, now and forever. [156]

p. 51.1, Old Gallican

O Christ,
receive our prayers,
and bless us this coming holy night of Easter,
that we may rise from the dead
and pass over into life with you,
Savior of the world. [157]

p. 51.2, Old Gallican

Hear us,
never-fading Light, Lord our God,
our only Light, Fountain of light,
Light of your angels,

thrones, dominions, principalities, powers,
and of all intelligent beings.
You created the light of your saints.
May our souls be your lamps,
kindled and enlightened by you.
May they shine and burn with the truth,
and never go out in darkness and ashes.
May we be your house,
shining from you, shining in you.
May we shine without fail.
May we ever worship you.
In you may we be kindled and not be extinguished.
Being filled with the splendor
of your Son, our Lord Jesus Christ,
may we shine forth inwardly.
May the gloom of sins be cleared away,
and the light of constant faith abide within us. [158]

p. 52.1, Mozarabic, blessing of the Paschal candle on Easter Eve, also Gregorian

It is truly good and right,
with all powers of heart and mind,
and with the service of our lips,
to praise the invisible God,
the Father almighty, and his only Son
our Lord Jesus Christ,
who paid the debt of Adam for us to the eternal Father,
and erased the stain of ancient guilt
by his blood poured out in love.
For this is the Paschal festival
in which Christ, the true Lamb was slain,
and the door-posts hallowed by his blood,
by which you first brought our ancestors,
the children of Israel, out of Egypt,
and led them through the Red Sea with dry feet.
This is the night
which cleared away the darkness of sin with a pillar of light.
This is the night
which restores grace and unites believers in Christ
in holiness throughout the world,
separated from worldly vices and from the gloom of sin.
This the night
in which Christ broke the bonds of death
and ascended from the grave as a Conqueror.
Life itself would be no blessing to us
without his redemption.
O wondrous love!

To redeem your servants you gave up your Son.
This holy night,
drives off offences, washes away sins,
restores innocence to the fallen and joy to the sad.
O truly blessed night,
which spoiled the Egyptians and enriched the Hebrews —
the night in which heaven and earth are reconciled!
We pray therefore, O Lord,
that you would preserve your servants
in the peace and joy of this Easter happiness;
through Jesus Christ our Lord. [159]

p. 52.2, Gregorian

The time has come that we have longed for.
What greater or better work can be found
than to proclaim the might of our risen Lord?
Bursting open the doors of the grave,
he has displayed to us the glorious banner of his resurrection.
Through him the children of light are born to life eternal,
the courts of the kingdom of heaven are opened to believers,
and by God's own decree the earthly and heavenly are brought together.
By the cross of Christ, we have all been redeemed from death,
and by his resurrection our life has been restored.
While he has assumed our mortal nature,
we acknowledge him as the God of majesty,
and in the glory of the Godhead
we confess him God and Man.
By dying he destroyed our death,
and by rising again restored our life;
Jesus Christ our Lord. [160]

p. 54.1, Gelasian, Easter Preface

O God,
you overcame death by your only Son
and opened the gate of eternal life for us.
By the celebration of our Lord's resurrection,
renew us by your Spirit and raise us from the death of the soul;
through the same Jesus Christ our Lord. [161]

p. 54.2, Gregorian / Gelasian / Gothic

O almighty God,
hear your people,
who glorify the resurrection of your Son our Lord.
Guide them on from this festival to eternal gladness,
from the joy of this celebration to joys that have no end.
For this is the day of humanity's resurrection,
the birthday of eternal life,
in which we have been satisfied
with your mercy in the morning,
in which the blessed One
who comes in the name of the Lord,
who is our God, has shined on us. [162]

p. 55.1, Gothic Missal

O Lord,
preserve with watchful love
those you have cleansed,
that those who have been redeemed by your Passion
may rejoice in your resurrection. [163]

p. 55.2, Gelasian

O God,
you sacrificed your Son as the Lamb of God for the world's salvation.[17]
Hear our prayers,
for our supreme High Priest,
intercedes for us and reconciles us because he became like us,
and he absolves us because he is equal to you;
Jesus Christ our Lord, who with you and the Holy Spirit
lives and reigns, God forever. [164]

p. 55.3, Gelasian

O God,
in your Son's suffering you gave us a solution for sin and death[18]
that remains with your people as your most precious gift.
Let what we delight in now be our joy forever;
through Jesus Christ our Lord. [165]

p. 55.4, Gelasian

O Lord,
blot out the handwriting made by the law of sin.
You cancelled it by the suffering and resurrection of your Son,[19]
Jesus Christ our Lord. [166]

p. 56.1, Gelasian

---

[17] Original translation: "O God, Who hast appointed the Paschal Sacrifice for the world's salvation,..."
[18] Original translation: "O God, Who hast bestowed upon us the Paschal remedy,..."
[19] Original translation: " ...which Thou hast made void in us by the Paschal mystery,"

O Lord,
in the death and resurrection of your Son,[20]
teach us to scorn earthly desires,
and to long after heavenly things;
through Jesus Christ our Lord. [167]

p. 56.2, Gelasian

O merciful God,
grant that in the resurrection of our Lord Jesus Christ
we may have our inheritance;
through the same our Lord. [168]

p. 56.3, Gelasian

Almighty God,
grant that we who celebrate the Paschal festival
may always live in your sanctifying grace;
through Jesus Christ our Lord. [169]

p. 56.4, Gregorian

O God,
by the Paschal festival
you have given healing gifts on the world.
Bless your people,
that they may enjoy perfect freedom,
and advance to eternal life;
through Jesus Christ our Lord. [170]

p. 56.5, Gregorian

Almighty and eternal God,
you brought about your Son's resurrection
to complete humanity's reconciliation.[21]
Grant to our souls,
that what we celebrate by our profession
we may imitate in our practice;
through Jesus Christ our Lord. [171]

p. 56.6, Gregorian

O God,
by Christ's resurrection
you restore us to eternal life.
Raise us up to the Author of our salvation
who is seated at your right hand,
that he who came to be judged for our sake
may come to judge in our favor;

---

[20] Original translation: "O Lord, be pleased by the Paschal remedies to grant unto us that we may learn..."
[21] Original translation: "Who hast vouchsafed the Paschal mystery in the covenant of man's reconciliation."

your Son, Jesus Christ our Lord,
who lives and reigns with you and the Holy Spirit,
one God, now and forever. [172]

p. 57.1, Gregorian

Almighty God,
help us put off the old man with his deeds and live in Christ,
whom you have shared with us by the healing gifts of Easter,
who lives and reigns with you and the Holy Spirit,
one God, now and forever. [173]

p. 57.2, Gregorian

O God,
you are the Author of our freedom and of our salvation.
Hear the voices of your people,
that those you redeemed by shedding your blood
may live in you, and always enjoy safety in you,
Savior of the world. [174]

p. 57.3, Gothic

O Lord,
just as we celebrate the mysteries of the resurrection of our Lord Jesus,
we may rejoice with all his saints when he comes again;
through the same Jesus Christ our Lord. [175]

p. 57.4, Old Gallican

Lamb of God,
you take away the sin of the world,
look on us and have mercy on us.
Victim and Priest,
Reward and Redeemer,
protect those you have redeemed from all evil,
Savior of the world. [176]

p. 58.1, Old Gallican

We give you thanks,
God the Father,
for delivering us from the power of darkness,
and bringing us into the kingdom of your Son.
Grant that as he has recalled us to life by his death,
he may raise us up in his love to joys eternal. [177]

p. 58.2, Mozarabic

Only Son of God,
you willingly shed your blood for us and reconciled earth and heaven.
As we worship you
and remember the mystery of our redemption and your resurrection,
give us your never-ending peace. [178]

p. 58.3, Mozarabic

O God the Father almighty,
you so loved the world
that you gave your only Son
to be crucified for our redemption.
Make us who are redeemed by his blood, fruitful in works of love,
that we may have our part in the first resurrection,
and not fear the power of the second death. [179]

p. 58.4, Mozarabic

Almighty God and Father,
with the precious blood of your Son
our Lord Jesus Christ,
you redeemed us.
Do not let those who believe
fall into the abyss of eternal punishment.
Grant that by confessing our sins
we may come into your presence through him,
on whom you laid the iniquity of us all.
As we are healed by his wounds,
may we also be defended by his protection. [180]

p. 59.1, Mozarabic

O Lord Jesus,
we confess that you died for sins which was not yours, but ours,
Since you died once for the ungodly, you live to God.
Make us to die to sin once,
that rising again to receive our crown
we may forever rejoice in your eternal gifts. [181]

p. 59.2, Mozarabic

Almighty God,
grant that we who have gone
through the Paschal festival
may be moved by your goodness
to keep it also by our conduct and life;
through Jesus Christ our Lord. [182]

p. 59.3, Gregorian

ASCENSION

O Lord,
hear our prayers.
Just as we trust
that the Savior of humanity
is seated with you in your majesty,
we may also trust that he remains with us always
to the end of the age, as he has promised;
through the same Jesus Christ our Lord. [183]

p. 59.4, Leonine

Almighty and eternal God,
bless us as we celebrate this day's festival
and direct our eyes heavenward
where in human flesh, your only Son is with you;
through the same Jesus Christ our Lord. [184]

p. 60.1, Leonine

Hear us, merciful God,
and lift our minds
where our Redeemer has ascended,
that at the second coming of our Mediator
we may receive from your goodness
what we now hope for as a promised gift;
through the same Jesus Christ our Lord. [185]

p. 60.2, Leonine

Almighty God,
lead the faithful members of your Son
to follow where our Head and Chief has gone before;
who lives and reigns with you and the Holy Spirit,
one God, now and forever. [186]

p. 60.3, Leonine

O God,
you showed the wonders of your majesty
after your resurrection from the dead
by ascending into heaven in the presence of your apostles.
Help us by your loving kindness,
and according to your promise,
dwell with us on earth
until we dwell with you in heaven;
where with the Father and the Holy Spirit
you live and reign,
one God, now and forever. [187]

p. 60.4, Leonine

O Lord,
you bore our weak flesh
and now you are glorified in heaven.
Take away the foulness of our sins
and restore the dignity of humanity
as it was in the beginning,
that by faith in you
our hearts may ascend
where we know you have ascended. [188]

p. 61.1, Mozarabic

Savior and Lord,
by ascending into heaven
you showed yourself in glory to your disciples,
and you also promised to come again
in the same way as you have gone into heaven.
Give us pure and devout hearts
as we celebrate your ascension,
that we may continually ascend to a better life in you,
that when you come in judgment
we may see your face
and not be put to shame. [189]

p. 61.2, Mozarabic

O God,
you have gone up on high
leading captivity captive.
Give us your gifts of eternal peace.
By ascending into heaven
you are now hidden from our sight.
In your grace, enter our hearts. [190]

p. 61.3, Mozarabic

WHITSUNTIDE (PENTECOST)

Almighty God,
shine on us with the splendor of your brightness,
and with the light of your Light
strengthen the hearts of those
who have been born again through your grace
with the illumination of the Holy Spirit;
for the sake of Jesus Christ our Lord. [191]

p. 61.4, Gregorian, Whitsun Eve

Almighty God,
grant that we who celebrate
the gift of your Holy Spirit
may be kindled with heavenly desires
and thirst for the fountain of life;
through Jesus Christ our Lord. [192]

p. 62.1, Gregorian, Whitsun Eve

Almighty and eternal God,
on this day you completed
the work of your Son's suffering, death and resurrection.[22]
Give us that peace our Lord Jesus Christ left to us
when he ascended to you;
through the same Jesus Christ our Lord. [193]

p. 62.2, Leonine

O Lord,
let the Holy Spirit
prepare our minds by divine mysteries,
for he himself is the remission of all sins;
through Jesus Christ our Lord. [194]

p. 62.3, Leonine

O Lord,
let the power of the Holy Spirit be present with us,
cleansing our hearts and protecting us in all trouble;
through our Lord Jesus Christ. [195]

p. 62.4, Leonine

O God,
by reminding us of your Spirit, his gifts and his work,[23]
you sanctify your universal Church in every race and nation.
Pour out on the whole world the gift of the Holy Spirit
that his good, divine work at the first preaching of the gospel
may be extended among believing hearts;
through Jesus Christ our Lord. [196]

p. 62.5, Gelasian

O God,
you sent on your disciples
the Holy Spirit, the Counselor,
in the burning fire of your love.
Give your people a loving unity of faith,
that abiding in you
they may be steadfast in faith and active in work;
through Jesus Christ our Lord. [197]

p. 63.1, Gelasian

O Lord,
may the Spirit, the Counselor,
who proceeds from you,
enlighten our minds
and lead us into all truth

---

[22] Original translation: "Who in the fulness of this day's mystery hast completed the secret work of the Paschal solemnity;"
[23] Original translation: "...by the mystery of this day's festival dost sanctify..."

as your Son has promised;
through the same our Lord Jesus Christ. [198]

p. 63.2, Gelasian

O Lord,
may the outpouring of the Holy Spirit,
cleanse our hearts and make them fruitful
like abundant dew from heaven;
through our Lord Jesus Christ. [199]

p. 63.3, Gelasian

O God
you gave your apostles the Holy Spirit.
Bless your people's devout prayer.
Just as you have given us faith, also give us peace;
through Jesus Christ our Lord. [200]

p. 63.4, Gelasian

O Lord,
let the Holy Spirit light in us
that fire our Lord Jesus Christ sent to the earth,
and eagerly desired to see kindled;[24]
who lives and reigns with you and the Holy Spirit,
one God, now and forever. [201]

p. 63.5, Gregorian

O God,
Enlightener and Life of believers,
we celebrate your great gifts on this day's festival.
Help your people understand
that they are your adopted children
whom the Holy Spirit has gathered
to have fervent love for you
and confess your faith in complete unity;
through Jesus Christ our Lord. [202]

p. 64.1, Gothic / Leonine

Holy God, Father almighty,
fill us with the gift of your only Son,
and the wonderful blessing, visitation, and life-giving power
of the Holy Spirit, who proceeds from him and you.
Enkindle your church with his fire,
that it may hold the true faith in you
from whom it receives all truth. [203]

p. 64.2, Mozarabic

---

[24] Luke 12:49

O Lord,
let your mercy be on us,
and let the brightness of your Spirit
enlighten our inward souls,
that he may kindle our cold hearts
and light up our dark minds,
who abides forever with you in glory. [204]

p. 64.3, Mozarabic

O Holy Spirit,
you proceed from the Father and the Son.
Teach us your truth
and unite us in a bond of holy love
to the Father and Son,
from whom you proceed. [205]

p. 65.1, Mozarabic

O Lord,
send your Holy Spirit among us,
wash us with the pure water of repentance,
and prepare us to be living sacrifices to you. [206]

p. 65.2, Mozarabic

Heavenly King, Counselor, Spirit of Truth,
you are present everywhere and fill all things.
You are the treasury of good and giver of life.
Come and dwell in us,
purify us from every stain,
and save our souls
in your goodness. [207]

p. 65.3, Midnight Office of the Eastern Church

TRINITY SUNDAY

O Lord God,
Father almighty,
bless and protect your servants
who are obedient to your majesty
through your only Son,
in the power of the Holy Spirit.
Free them from fear of all enemies
that they may continually rejoice in praising you;
through the same Jesus Christ our Lord. [208]

p. 65.4, Gregorian, Trinity

Lord Jesus Christ,
pour into us the Holy Spirit
promised by the Father,
that he may give us life
and teach us the fullness of truth
in the mystery of the blessed and undivided Trinity,
since our salvation is perfectly accomplished
by his complete and powerful gift. [209]

p. 66.1, Mozarabic

O Holy Spirit,
Comforter,
with the Father and the Son
you are one God in Trinity.
Come to our hearts
and make intercession for us
that we may call on our Father
with full confidence. [210]

p. 66.2, Mozarabic

May the infinite and wonderful Trinity,
the Father, the Son, and the Holy Spirit,
direct our lives in good works,
and after our passage through this world
give us eternal rest with the righteous.
Grant this, O eternal and almighty God. [211]

p. 66.3, Mozarabic

O Lord,
Savior and Guardian of those who fear you,
turn this world's deceptive wisdom
away from your Church.
With your Spirit
instruct and delight us
in the words of the prophets
and the teaching of the apostles
and turn us from the world's empty philosophy,
so that the darkness of falsehood
may not deceive those enlightened by your truth;
through Jesus Christ our Lord. [212]

p. 66.4, Gelasian

Blessed and glorious Trinity,
Father, Son, and Holy Spirit,
thanks to you,
true and single Trinity,
one and perfect Godhead.
You, God the Father unbegotten,
you, the one and only Son,
you, the Holy Spirit and Counselor,
holy and undivided Trinity,
we confess and praise you
with heart and mouth.
To you be glory forever. Alleluia! [213]

p. 67.1, Sarum Sunday Office, after the Athanasian Creed

SAINTS' DAYS

O God,
you are the strength of all your saints,
and in your goodness and grace
you brought them to their present glory.
Pardon our sins
and enable us to remember and imitate their lives;[25]
through Jesus Christ our Lord. [214]

p. 67.2, Leonine

O Lord our God,
multiply your grace on us,
and help us follow your people
who gloriously struggled for the faith
and triumphed in you;
through Jesus Christ our Lord. [215]

p. 67.3, Leonine

Almighty God,
grant that we may always praise you
when we remember your saints.
You will care for and protect
those you enabled to persevere in love for you;
through Jesus Christ our Lord. [216]

p. 68.1, Leonine

---

[25] Original translation: "...sins, that we may be able worthily to celebrate their solemnities;"

54

Almighty and eternal God,
you empowered your saints
not only to believe in your Son,
but also to suffer for his sake.
Help us also in our weakness,
that as they gave up their lives
hoping in your eternal mercy,
we may at last receive your hope
by sincerely confessing you;
through Jesus Christ our Lord. [217]

p. 68.2, Leonine

Almighty and eternal God,
you adorn the sacred body of your Church
by the confessions of holy martyrs.
Help us to follow both their teaching and example,
and do what is pleasing in your sight;
through Jesus Christ our Lord. [218]

p. 68.3, Leonine

Merciful Lord,
increase our faith in you.
As faith brought your holy martyrs to glory,
who remained faithful, even with shedding their blood,
it may also justify us who follow it in truth;
through Jesus Christ our Lord. [219]

p. 68.4, Leonine

O Lord our God,
as we welcome this day
and remember your saints,
may we also rejoice
when we see them in your presence eternally;[26]
through Jesus Christ our Lord. [220]

p. 69.1, Leonine

Almighty God,
let the examples of your saints
encourage us toward a better life,
so that we who celebrate their festivals
may also imitate their actions;
through Jesus Christ our Lord. [221]

p. 69.2, Leonine

---

[26] Original translation did not have "in your presence."

O God,
today we remember all your saints.
Bring us together with them
to enjoy your eternal fellowship and gladness;
through Jesus Christ our Lord. [222]

p. 69.3, Gregorian

Almighty and eternal God,
you enkindle the flame of your love
in the hearts of the saints.
Give us the same power of faith and love
that we may learn from their examples
and rejoice in their victory
through Jesus Christ our Lord. [223]

p. 69.4, Gothic

O God,
you have enkindled
in the hearts of your saints
such great faith
that they forgot all bodily pains
while holding on in faith
until they departed to you, the Author of life.
Hear our prayers,
and grant that the hateful attraction of sin may flicker out in us,
and we may glow with the infused warmth of love for you;
through your mercy, O our God,
you are blessed,
and live and govern all things,
now and forever. [224]

p. 70.1, Mozarabic

O Christ, Son of God,
our great joy and eternal gladness,
after their bitter sufferings
you give your saints
the sweet vision of your glory,
so that pain and groaning
have no more place among them.
Give us also
the healing gift of comfort,
that we who have gone astray like sheep
may be gathered into the company of your saints,
and with them receive your unending joy;
through your mercy, O our God,

you are blessed,
and live and govern all things,
now and forever. [225]

p. 70.2, Mozarabic

DURING TRINITY TIME
PRAYERS FOR VARIOUS GRACES

1. For Conversion of Will to God.

Almighty and eternal God,
convert us completely to yourself.
As you give your good gifts to the undeserving,
bestow even greater gifts on those who trust in you;
through Jesus Christ our Lord. [226]

p. 70.3, Leonine

Almighty and eternal God,
convert our minds
to do what is pleasing to you,
Do not let your rebuke be met with our neglect,
and become a greater reason for punishment,
but let your Fatherly admonition be a blessing
as we amend our lives;
through Jesus Christ our Lord. [227]

p. 71.1, Leonine

O Lord,
convert all our hearts to yourself,
that we abstain from whatever offends you,
and experience your mercy and not your wrath;
through Jesus Christ our Lord. [228]

p. 71.2, Leonine

Eternal Father,
convert our hearts to yourself,
for those you move
to your devotion and worship
will lack no good thing;
through Jesus Christ our Lord. [229]

p. 71.3, Leonine

Almighty God, do not look on our many evils,
but draw us away from sin, for we are weak,
and guide our wills to what is right;
through Jesus Christ our Lord. [230]

p. 71.4, Leonine

O Lord our God,
your compassion is what has moved us
to fear and love your name.
In mercy pour your grace into our hearts,
that we cast away everything that displeases you,
and become united to you with an honest will;
through Jesus Christ our Lord. [231]

p. 71.5, Leonine

O God,
Comforter of the humble
and Strength of the faithful,
be merciful to your people.
Strengthen our weakness
so that we may stand before you;
through Jesus Christ our Lord. [232]

p. 72.1, Gelasian

O God,
you give peace
and you love charity.
Give your servants
a true agreement with your will,
that we may be delivered
from all the temptations that attack us;
through Jesus Christ our Lord. [233]

p. 72.2, Gelasian

O Lord,
you have healed our wounds
by the wounds of your only Son.
What then should we do
since we have been bought at so great a price?
How shall we serve such a Lord
who has promised such liberty
and has offered such an inheritance to us?
O Lord, work in us what pleases you.
Possess us so that we may possess you.
We will not die but live,
and we will call on your name. [234]

p. 72.3, Mozarabic

2.   For the Fear of God.

Deliver us from evil,
and strengthen us to fear you and do good works,
O Trinity, our God,
you are blessed,

and live and govern all things,
now and forever. [235]

p. 73.1, Mozarabic

O God,
by the prophet's voice
you pronounce those blessed who fear you.
Work a holy fear and obedience in us
that we may walk in your ways,
and direct our work
to be pleasing in your sight,
and let its fruit be sweet in the day of your reward. [236]

p. 73.2, Mozarabic

3.   For Humility.

Almighty and eternal God,
you resist the proud
and give grace to the humble.
Grant that we may not exalt ourselves
and provoke your anger,
but bow down
and receive the gifts of your mercy;
through Jesus Christ our Lord. [237]

p. 73.3, Mozarabic

O God,
by your will all things were made,
and by your truth they continue to exist.
Keep us under your protection
so that we do not forfeit our chief happiness
by arrogance and pride.
Lead us in your heavenly way
to follow your humility.
You are the Fountain of life.
May we drink from you and never thirst again.
In your light may we shine
with the light of knowledge
and reap the fruit of righteousness
in eternal joy. [238]

p. 73.4, Mozarabic

O God,
you are rich in forgiveness,
and you took on our lowly flesh
to leave us an example of humility
and make us steadfast in all kinds of suffering.
Help us always to hold on to the good things we receive from you,
and as often as we fall into sins,
lead us to repentance and raise us up;
through your mercy. [239]

p. 74.1, Gothic Missal

4. For Faith.

O Lord,
in your compassion
increase our faith in you.
In your loving-kindness
you help those you have given
steadfast faith in you;
through Jesus Christ our Lord. [240]

p. 74.2, Leonine

O Lord,
lead us to trust in you with all our heart.
Since you always resist the proud
who trust in their own strength,
do not forsake those who boast in your mercy;
through Jesus Christ our Lord. [241]

p. 74.3, Leonine

O Lord,
confirm in our minds
the mysteries of the true faith,
that as we confess Christ
who was conceived by the virgin
to be true God and fully human,
so by the power of his saving resurrection
we may receive eternal joy;
through the same Jesus Christ our Lord. [242]

p. 75.1, Gregorian

Be gracious and hear our prayers,
O merciful God,
and in love, protect your people,
that those who confess your only Son
as God born in human flesh
may never be corrupted

by the deceits of the devil;
through the same Jesus Christ our Lord. [243]

p. 75.2, Ambrosian

O God,
you are One and True.
We humbly pray
that the true Christian faith
may continue forever in us all;
through Jesus Christ our Lord. [244]

p. 75.3, Gallican

Lord Jesus Christ,
true God and fully human,
you do not change,
and you are holy in all your works.
Remove all our unbelief and doubt,
and fill our hearts with the gifts of your grace
that we may believe and know you as true God,
and by your miracles and mighty works
know you as Savior of all. [245]

p. 75.4, Mozarabic, Easter 4

O Lord,
always strengthen us
with sincere faith in your incarnation;
Establish us in your love,
that the crafty enemy
may never overcome us. [246]

p. 75.5, Mozarabic

Arise, O Lord,
Judge of all the earth.
Since you are the light who enlightens the Gentiles,
do not allow us to remain in darkness.
Establish the foundation of our faith
on you, our steadfast rock,
not on the sand
where wind and wave
will overcome it. [247]

p. 76.1, Mozarabic

5.   *For Hope*

It is good for us to cling to you, O Lord,
but increase our desire for your good,
that our hope in you may not be shaken by any wavering of faith,
but may endure in your steadfast love. [248]

p. 76.2, Mozarabic

May the hope you have given us, O Lord,
be our comfort when we are sorrowful
and our glory when we rejoice. [249]

p. 76.3, Mozarabic

Merciful Lord,
Comforter and Teacher of your faithful people,
increase in your Church the desires you have given.
Strengthen the hearts of those who hope in you,
and show them the depth of your promises.
Lead all your adopted children to see with the eyes of faith,
and help them wait patiently for the light that is now hidden;
through Jesus Christ our Lord. [250]

p. 76.4, Ambrosian

6.   For Love.

O God,
you have taught your Church
to keep all your heavenly commandments
by loving you and our neighbor.
Give us your Spirit of peace and grace
that we may be devoted to you with all our hearts
and united to each other with a purified will;
through Jesus Christ our Lord. [251]

p. 77.1, Leonine

O Lord,
strengthen the hearts of your children
with the power of your grace
that they may be devout in prayer to you
and sincere in love for each other;
through Jesus Christ our Lord. [252]

p. 77.2, Leonine

O God,
you make all things work together
for good to those who love you.
Fill us with the invincible power of your love
that the holy desires you have put in our hearts
may not be changed by any temptation;
through Jesus Christ our Lord. [253]

p. 77.3, Gelasian

O Lord,
give strength to those who seek you,
and continually give them the holy desire to seek you,
that those who long to see your face
may not crave the world's empty pleasure. [254]

p. 78.1, Mozarabic

Abba, Father,
be a tender Father toward us your servants.
Govern, protect, preserve,
sanctify, guide, and console us.
Let us be so warmed with love for you
that we may never forget you,
most merciful Lord, most tender Father;
for Jesus Christ's sake. [255]

p. 78.2, Old Gallican Sacramentary

7. For Sacred Knowledge.

Let the light of your face shine on us, O Lord,
that your Word may go forth
and give light and understanding
to nourish the hearts of the simple.
Set our desires on your commandments
so that we may receive with open hearts
the Spirit of wisdom and understanding. [256]

p. 78.3, Mozarabic

O God,
you are the well of life,
and in your light we see light.
Shine the light of your holy knowledge on us
and show us your flowing fountain.
Give our thirsty souls living water
and shine your light from heaven on our darkened minds. [257]

p. 78.4, Mozarabic

8. For Heavenly Mindedness.

Almighty and merciful God,
we rise to your eternal blessedness,
not by the weakness of the flesh
but by the activity of the soul.
With the living breath of your Spirit
move us always to seek after the courts of the heavenly City,
and finally enter them with confidence, by your mercy;
through Jesus Christ our Lord. [258]

p. 79.1, Leonine

O Lord,
you teach us not to worry about earthly things,
but to love heavenly things.
Even now,
while we live among things that are passing away,
help us cling to those things that will remain forever;
through Jesus Christ our Lord. [259]

p. 79.2, Leonine

O Lord,
turn our hearts to your Word,
and turn them away from empty things.
Separate us from the love of earthly things
and unite our desires to things above. [260]

p. 79.3, Mozarabic

9. For Peace.

O eternal Son,
you abide forever.
You are of one being with the Father,
equal to him as Ruler and Creator.
Without being changed,
you assumed our flesh,
and being made fully human,
like us in every way, except without sin,
you became our Mediator with the Father.
You broke down the barrier
and reconciled the earthly with the heavenly,
making the two one by your incarnation.
You said to your holy apostles and disciples,
"My peace I give to you."
Give us now that peace, O Lord. [261]

p. 79.4, Coptic Liturgy of St. Gregory Theologus

O God of love,
giver of concord,
through your only Son
you have given us a new commandment
that we should love one another
even as you have loved us,
the unworthy and the wandering,
and gave your beloved Son for our life and salvation.
Lord, in our time of life on earth
give us a mind forgetful of past ill-will,
a pure conscience and sincere thoughts,
and hearts to love one another. [262]

p. 80.1, Coptic Liturgy of St. Cyril

God, you are the bottomless well of peace,
the heavenly sea of love,
the fountain of blessings,
and the giver of affection,
and you send peace to those who receive it.
Open to us this day the sea of your love,
and water us with the flowing streams of your grace.
Make us children of quietness, and heirs of peace.

Enkindle the fire of your love in us.
Plant holy reverence for you in us.
Strengthen our weakness by your power.
Bind us closely to you and to each other
in one firm bond of unity;
for the sake of Jesus Christ.[27] [263]

p. 80.2, Syrian Clementine Liturgy

God the Father,
source of Divinity,
good beyond all that is good,
fair beyond all that is fair,
in you is calmness, peace and unity.
Repair the things that divide us from each other
and restore our unity of love
like your divine love.
And as you are above all things,
unite us in goodness and love
that we may be spiritually one,
with you and with each other,
through your peace which makes all things peaceful
and through the grace, mercy, and tenderness
of your only Son. [264]

p. 81.1, Jacobite Liturgy of St. Dionysius

O Lord, always keep us in peace,
as you have given us confidence in you;
through Jesus Christ our Lord. [265]

p. 81.2, Gelasian

Let us pass our days in your peace,
rescue us from eternal condemnation,
and add us to the flock of your elect. [266]

p. 81.3, Gregorian

O Christ,
Word of the most high Father,
you were made flesh to dwell among us.
Enter our hearts,
that we who have been redeemed
by the mystery of your incarnation
may always remain united in the fellowship of peace. [267]

p. 82.1, Mozarabic

---

[27] "for the sake of Jesus Christ" added.

Lord God almighty,
Christ, King of glory,
you are our true Peace and Love eternal.
Enlighten our souls
with the brightness of your peace,
and purify our consciences
with the sweetness of your love,
that with peaceful hearts
we wait for the Author of peace.
Guard and protect us always
in the troubles of this world,
and being surrounded by your care,
draw us to be devoted to the love of your peace. [268]

p. 82.2, Mozarabic

O God,
in your great love for this world,
you reconciled earth to heaven
through your only Son.
Grant that we
who are hindered by the darkness of sin
from loving sincerely
may be filled with your goodness
by your light poured into our souls,
and embrace our friends in you,
and our enemies for your sake,
in a bond of mutual affection. [269]

p. 82.3, Mozarabic

O God, you are peace eternal.
Your gift is peace.
You have taught us
that your children will be called peacemakers.
Pour out your peace into our souls
that all discord may vanish away,
and that we may forever love and seek
the things that bring your peace;
through Jesus Christ our Lord. [270]

p. 82.4, Mozarabic

10. For Deliverance from Temptation.

Almighty and eternal God,
empower your church
to reject all deadly pleasures
and rejoice in your eternal salvation;
through Jesus Christ our Lord. [271]

p. 83.1, Leonine

O Lord,
renew your people inwardly and outwardly.
Do not let them be distracted by bodily pleasures,
make them vigorous with spiritual purpose,
and refresh that purpose with what is for this time,
that they may cling to what is eternal;
through Jesus Christ our Lord. [272]

p. 83.2, Leonine

O Lord,
protect your people,
strengthen their weakness,
and wash away their earthly stains.
While they walk
through the darkness of this mortal life,
refresh them by your light,
deliver them from all evils,
and grant them your mercy
to receive your highest blessing;
through Jesus Christ our Lord. [273]

p. 83.4, Leonine

In your mercy and majesty, O Lord,
look at your household,
that they may neither be stained with vices of their own,
nor held in bondage by the sins of others,
but be freed and cleansed from both
they may serve you;
through Jesus Christ our Lord. [274]

p. 84.1, Leonine

Hear us,
O Lord our God,
and separate the hearts of your faithful people
from the evils of the world,
that those who call you Lord with their own voice
may not fall back into the service of the devil;
through Jesus Christ our Lord. [275]

p. 84.2, Leonine

Almighty God,
as we press onwards in your way with devout minds,
help us escape the snares of the sins that oppress us;
through Jesus Christ our Lord. [276]

p. 84.3, Leonine

O Lord,
be with your people
as they walk through the snares of a wicked world,
and protect us in our weakness with your unfailing love;
through Jesus Christ our Lord. [277]

p. 84.4, Gelasian

O God,
you protected Shadrach, Meshach and Abednego
from the flames of fire.
We pray that we may not be burned by the flame of sins;
through Jesus Christ our Lord. [278]

p. 84.5, Leonine

O God,
you dwell in the hearts of the holy
and you do not forsake your faithful people.
Deliver us from earthly desires and fleshly appetites
that no sin may reign in us,
but that we may with serve you with free spirits as our only Lord;
through Jesus Christ. [279]

p. 85.1, Gelasian

11. For Purity.

O Lord,
pour out the Spirit of grace on your family,
and drive away from them any evil they may have done
when tempted by the lies of the devil or by worldly corruption,
that being cleansed inwardly and outwardly,
they may worship you in purity
and receive what they ask;
through Jesus Christ our Lord. [280]

p. 85.2, Leonine

O Lord,
be gracious to your people,
that they reject the things that displease you
and love your commandments.
Support them with your comfort in this mortal life
and bring them to the full enjoyment of life immortal;
through Jesus Christ our Lord. [281]

p. 85.3, Leonine

O Lord,
make us flourish like pure lilies
in the courts of your house,
and make us display to your people
the fragrance of good works
and the example of a godly life;

through your mercy, O our God,
you are blessed,
and live and govern all things,
now and forever. [282]

p. 85.4, Mozarabic

O God,
you always love what is true,
and you bring to light what is hidden.
You were pleased to humble yourself to be born of a virgin
for the world's salvation.
Sprinkle us with the hyssop of your Word
and purify us from our iniquities.
Mercifully pour into our souls
a right spirit to call on you;
through your mercy, O our God,
you are blessed,
and live and govern all things,
now and forever. [283]

p. 86.1, Mozarabic

12. For Guidance.

O Lord,
hear the prayers of your family,
and while they submit to you with all their hearts,
prosper, support, and surround them,
that following you as their Guide
they may be entangled in no evils
and be refilled with all good;
through Jesus Christ our Lord. [284]

p. 86.2, Leonine

O Lord,
in your loving-kindness,
set our life and behavior in order,
that no troubles overcome us
and that we lack no good thing;
through Jesus Christ our Lord. [285]

p. 86.3, Leonine

O God,
you are the Author and giver of every blessing.
Guide us on your path of righteousness
that we seek the testimonies of your law with pious hearts,
continually love what you command,
and desire the goal where they lead;
through Jesus Christ our Lord. [286]

p. 86.4, Gelasian

O Lord,
make us obedient to your commandments,
that we may prosper
as we follow the Author of our whole life;
through Jesus Christ our Lord. [287]

p. 87.1, Gelasian

O Lord,
give us pardon for our sins,
comfort in life,
and constant guidance
that we may faithfully serve you
and always receive your mercy;
through Jesus Christ our Lord. [288]

p. 87.2, Gelasian

Jesus our Master,
walk with us on the road
as we yearn to reach the heavenly country,
so that following your light,
we may stay on the way of righteousness
and never wander in the horrible darkness of this world's night
while you, the way, the truth, and the life,
are shining within us. [289]

p. 87.3, Mozarabic

O Lord,
our support and our refuge,
deliver us from temptation,
defend and save us,
uphold us with your right hand,
teach us by your discipline,
and keep our way and our life pure. [290]

p. 87.4, Mozarabic

O Christ,
guide us in your way
and in your mercy
show the fountain of wisdom to our thirsty minds
that we may drink the sweetness of eternal life
and be freed from the heaviness of sorrow. [291]

p. 88.1, Mozarabic

O Lord,
our redemption.
Be our protection.
Direct our minds by your gracious presence.
Watch over our paths
and guide us with your love

through the hidden snares of life.
Fix our hearts on you as we go forward,
and following in faith,
arrive at your goal. [292]

p. 88.2, Mozarabic

13. For Contentment.

O Lord,
bless your family,
that they may devote themselves to your service,
confide in your protection,
and receive what they humbly ask of you.
Defend them and give them rest
that they may not be left alone or helpless,
but be prepared for your eternal blessings;
through Jesus Christ our Lord. [293]

p. 88.3, Leonine

O Lord,
protect your people who trust in your mercy.
Cleanse them from the stain of sin,
that they may continue in holy living.
Give them all they need for body and life,
and finally give them the inheritance you have promised;
through Jesus Christ our Lord. [294]

p. 88.4, Leonine

O Lord,
help us always
to seek your kingdom and righteousness.
Mercifully give us all other things we need as well;
through Jesus Christ our Lord. [295]

p. 89.1, Gelasian

O God,
you have forbidden us
to be anxious about what we need for this life.
Move our hearts to seek you and your kingdom,
that all good things may be given to us as well;
through Jesus Christ our Lord. [296]

p. 89.2, Gelasian

14. For Spiritual Joy.

O Lord,
let your constant mercy remain with your church.
While your people endure the storms of this world,
refresh them with gladness,
and let them see the brightness of eternal bliss;
through Jesus Christ our Lord. [297]

p. 89.3, Leonine

O Lord our God,
let us always rejoice in our devotion to you.
When we serve the Author of all good,
our joy will be constant and complete;
through Jesus Christ our Lord. [298]

p. 89.4 Leonine

O Lord,
let your faithful people
rejoice in your blessings.
As they follow your commands,
may they please you in their lives
and happily receive the good things they pray for;
through Jesus Christ our Lord. [299]

p. 90.1, Leonine

O almighty God,
grant that we may obtain
the fullness of joy
and always be devoted
to your majesty;
through Jesus Christ our Lord. [300]

p. 90.2, Leonine

Lord,
pour into our hearts
the joy of your righteousness,
that in praising you
we may purge all unholiness from our minds;
through your mercy, O our God,
you are blessed,
and live and govern all things,
now and forever. [301]

p. 90.3, Mozarabic

15. For Thankfulness.

O God,
you discipline us in your love,
and you refresh us while we undergo your discipline.
Move us to give you thanks for both;
through Jesus Christ our Lord. [302]

p. 90.4, Leonine

Almighty God,
do not let prosperity
distract us from worshiping you,
but let it move us

to give deeper thanks to you;
through Jesus Christ our Lord. [303]

p. 90.5, Leonine

16. *For Recovery of Lost Happiness.*

O merciful God,
humanity fell away
from the happiness of Paradise
by violating your divine law.
Grant that we may
keep your commandments
and receive access to eternal bliss
in Jesus Christ our Lord. [304]

p. 91.1, Leonine

17. *For the help from the Angels.*

O God,
you order all things in heaven and earth
for the help of humanity.
As we work here on earth,
mercifully protect us by your angels from heaven;
through Jesus Christ our Lord. [305]

p. 91.2, Leonine

O Light from Light,
Brightness indescribable,
Christ our God,
Wisdom, Power, and Glory of the Father,
you appeared visibly to all as the Word made flesh,
and after you overcame the prince of darkness
you returned to your throne on high.
As your people live in this dark world,
show the glory of your rule,
and defend all our comings and goings
by the service of your holy angels,
and finally give us a place at your right hand
to receive the crown of life from you. [28] [306]

p. 91.3, Mozarabic

---

[28] "As your people..." Original translation: "grant to us Thy suppliants, amid this dark
world, the full outpouring of Thy splendour; appoint the Archangel Michael to be our defender, to guard
our going out and coming in;"

18. *For Perseverance.*

O God,
in your loving-kindness
you begin and finish all good things.
As we glory in the beginning of your grace,
so may we rejoice in its completion;
through Jesus Christ our Lord. [307]

p. 92.1, Leonine

Almighty and eternal God,
your paths are always mercy and truth.
Just as you nurture us by your tenderness,
help us grow with an increase of devotion;
through Jesus Christ our Lord. [308]

p. 92.2, Leonine

O God,
your gate of mercy
stands open to the faithful.
Look on us with mercy
as we follow the path of your will,
and let us never turn aside
from your path of life;
through Jesus Christ our Lord. [309]

p. 92.3, Gelasian

O God,
you have blessed us by your grace
and you have made us righteous instead of ungodly,
blessed instead of miserable.
Be with us,
and give perseverance
to all you have given faith;
through Jesus Christ our Lord. [310]

p. 92.4 Old Gallican

Look on us and hear us,
O Lord our God,
and help us to do what pleases you
as you have shown us.
As you give us the first spark of will,
bring our work to completion
that we may finish
what you let us begin. [311]

p. 93.1, Mozarabic

Hear our prayer, O Lord,
and let our cries come before you.
Do not cut us off in the midst of our life,

but let us finish our course of holy living,
like those who can see the goal.
And after pursuing a holy life during the time you give us,
welcome us into your eternal kingdom of glory. [312]

p. 93.2, Mozarabic

O God,
    set us on fire with your Spirit.
    Strengthen us with your power.
    Enlighten us with your splendor.
    Fill us with your grace.
    Draw us forward with your help.
O Lord, give us
    a right faith, perfect love, true humility.
O Lord, give us
    simple affection, brave patience,
    persevering obedience,
    perpetual peace,
    a pure mind,
    a right and clean heart,
    a good will,
    a sharpened conscience,
    spiritual strength,
    a life unspotted and blameless.
And having finished the course,
enter your kingdom by your grace. [29] [313]

p. 93.3, Gallican Sacramentary

19. For a Happy Death.

O God,
you are the Savior of all the living
and do not desire the death of sinners
or rejoice in the death of the wicked.
Pardon my offences,
that I may confess the sins I have committed
and commit them no more.
When my last day
and the end of my life arrive,
let your holy angel receive me
cleansed from all offences
through Jesus Christ our Lord. [314]

p. 94.1, Gallican Sacramentary

---

[29] "...by your grace" was added for doctrinal clarity.

O God of love and peace,
you endured the torture of the Cross,
and shed your blood for our redemption
for the salvation of humanity.
Graciously receive my prayers
and have mercy on me,
that when you command me to depart from the body,
the enemy may have no power over me,
but the angel of peace may place me
among your saints and elect,
where light abides and life reigns,
now and forever. [315]

p. 94.2, Gallican Sacramentary

20. For Mercy in the Judgment.

O Lord,
deliver me from eternal death
in that tremendous day
when the heavens and the earth will be shaken
and you come to judge the world by fire.
That day is a day of wrath,
of calamity and misery,
a great and very bitter day.
What should a sinner, such as I say or do,
when I have no good thing to bring before the awesome Judge?
O Christ, we appeal to you—pity us.
You came to redeem the lost and will not condemn the redeemed. [316]

p. 95.1, Sarum Office of the Dead

In that time of terror and of dread,
that time full of sadness,
have pity, O Lord,
on those who confess your Passion.
Protect those who put their trust
in your love for humanity,
and forgive their sins.
Let your tenderness be stirred up
for those who call on your holy name.
Your grace will not fail us.
Do not rebuke your servants for their filthy garments.
Do not let the light of our lamps go out.
Do not let your judgment be against us.
By your grace help us fight our wickedness.
Pity our waywardness.
Wash away our sins.
Erase whatever is hateful in us.
Give us true and uncorrupt faith,

a pure and tranquil life,
high and holy gifts,
freedom from severe temptations,
a departure with due preparation,
a good end, richest blessings,
lasting delights, inheritance with the saints,
and confidence when we stand before your awesome throne,
because you are merciful and rich in your goodness. [317]

p. 95.2, Syrian Clementine Liturgy

21. A General Prayer.

O Lord,
give me
    pure lips,
    a clean and innocent heart,
    and rightness of action.
Give me
    humility, patience, abstinence,
    chastity, prudence, justice,
    courage and self-control.
Give me
    the Spirit of wisdom and understanding,
    the Spirit of counsel and strength,
    the Spirit of knowledge and godliness,
    and of your fear.
Always lead me to seek your face
    with all my heart, all my soul, all my mind.
Let me have a contrite and humble heart in your presence—
    to prefer nothing to your love.
Most high, eternal, and wonderful Wisdom,
    drive away from me the darkness of blindness and ignorance.
Most high and eternal Strength, rescue me.
Most high and eternal Courage, help me.
Most high and incomprehensible Light, enlighten me,
Most high and infinite Mercy, have mercy on me. [318]

p. 96.1, Gallican, from the time of Charlemagne

INTERCESSIONS

1. For the Church.

O Lord,
mercifully hear the prayers of your Church.
Destroy all adversities and errors
that it may serve you in quiet freedom,
and us give your peace in our time;
through Jesus Christ our Lord. [319]

p. 97.1, Leonine / Sarum

O Lord,
in your loving-kindness
hear the cries of your Church.
Forgive our sins
that we may become devout by the working of your grace,
and tranquil under the protection of your power;
through Jesus Christ our Lord. [320]

p. 97.2, Leonine

O good Shepherd,
look mercifully on your flock,
and do not let
the sheep you redeemed with your precious blood
to be torn to pieces by the assaults of the devil. [321]

p. 97.3, Leonine

O God,
you promised
that you would be with your Church
to the end of the age,
and that the gates of hell
will never prevail against the apostolic confession.
Make your strength perfect in our weakness,
and keep your divine promise
and be present with your weakest members.
Give each of us what we ask, as it pleases you,
guard us from the attacks of all our enemies,
and assure us with your presence. [322]

p. 97.2, Leonine

Almighty and eternal God,
by Christ you revealed your glory to all nations.
Preserve the works of your mercy,
that your Church, which is spread throughout the world,
may persevere with steadfast faith
in the confession of your name;
through Jesus Christ our Lord. [323]

O God of unchangeable power and eternal light,
look favorably on your whole Church,
which is a wonderful and sacred mystery.
In your eternal foreknowledge,
you peacefully do your saving work for humanity.
Let the whole world know
that things that were cast down are being raised up,
and things that had grown old are being made new,
and all things are being restored by him
in whom they have their beginning;
Jesus Christ our Lord. [324]

p. 98.2, Gelasian, Holy Saturday

O God,
you restore and rule humanity.
Grant that your Church may grow in number,
and all the faithful increase in devotion;
through Jesus Christ our Lord. [325]

p. 99.1, Gelasian

O God,
you have made all those who are born again in Christ
to be your royal priesthood.
Grant us both the will and the power
to do what you command,
that your people who are called to eternal life
may have the same faith in their hearts,
and the same devotion in their actions;
through Jesus Christ our Lord [326]

p. 99.2, Gelasian

O almighty God,
your goodness is boundless,
and you are to be feared for your mercy.
Help us, and drive away all the trials
of earthly sin and worldly danger,
so that in your Christian Church
pure religious devotion may always continue;
through Jesus Christ our Lord. [327]

p. 99.3, Leonine

O Lord,
always guide and govern your Church
that it may walk carefully in times of quiet
and boldly in times of trouble;
through our Lord. [328]

p. 100.1, Francic (Northern Gaul)

O Lord,
let your Word, which endures forever in heaven,
remain also in the Temple of your Church,
that your presence may be a constant glory for your people;
through your mercy, O our God,
you are blessed,
and live and govern all things,
now and forever. [329]

p. 100.2, Mozarabic

Remember your congregation, O Lord,
which you created from the beginning.
Do not forget your Church
which you predestined in Christ
before the world began.
Remember your mercy,
look on your covenant,
and bless us continually
with the freedom you have promised. [330]

p. 100.3, Mozarabic

O Lord,
see how your faithful Jerusalem
rejoices in the triumph of the Cross
and the power of the Savior.
Grant that those who love her
may abide in her peace,
and those who depart from her
may one day come back to her.
When all sorrows are taken away,
refresh us with the joys of an eternal resurrection,
and share with us her peace now and forever;
through your mercy, O our God,
you are blessed,
and live and govern all things,
now and forever. [331]

p. 100.4, Mozarabic

2. For Bishops and Pastors.

O God,
by the power of your majesty
you determine the number of our days
and the measure of our time.
Accept our humble service,
and grant that our times,
and those of _____, our bishop,
may be filled with the abundance of your peace

and the grace of your goodness;
through Jesus Christ our Lord. [332]

p. 101.1, Gelasian

Lord Jesus Christ,
you chose your apostles
to preside over us as teachers.
Teach your doctrine to _____, our bishop,
in the place of your apostles,
and bless and instruct him,
that he may watch his life and doctrine closely,
and live unharmed under your blessing. [333]

p. 101.2, Pontifical of Egbert, d. 766

O Christ,
you are the true and eternal High Priest.
Help your servants with your power
and clothe them with glory and beauty,
that they may carefully and excellently
discharge their ministries as it pleases you.
Let them use the talents you have given them
as the Spirit gives ability.
When their work is done,
may they return their talents to you with interest,
and hear your voice full of hope,
"Enter into the joy that has no end."
O Lord, may they go from strength to strength.
Lift them up while they worship you.
Increase your gifts in them.
Crown their heads with your goodness,
and store up your grace their hearts.
Give them your abundant help,
and fill their labors with power. [334]

p. 101.3, Syro-Nestorian Ordinal

O God,
your ways are mercy and truth.
Carry on your gracious work,
and with your gifts
give us what our human weakness cannot attain,
that the stewards of your mysteries
may be grounded in perfect faith,
and shine like the brightness of the sky above
with lives lived to your glory;
through Jesus Christ our Lord. [335]

p. 102.1, Leonine

Lord God of hosts,
sanctify the pastors and shepherds of your sheep,
that our adversary the devil
may be overcome by their faith and holiness,
and not dare to touch or violate the flock of the Lord;
through the same our Lord Jesus Christ. [336]

p. 102.2, Gothic Missal

Several of the Prayers for the use of Clergy (see below) may be altered into an intercessory form.

3. For the Sovereign.

O God,
in your hand are the hearts of kings,
hear our prayer,
and with your wisdom govern our *King,*
your servant _____,
that *his* counsels may be drawn from your fountain,
and *he* may be well-pleasing in your sight,
and pre-eminent among all sovereigns;
through Jesus Christ our Lord. [337]

p. 103.1, Gelasian

Almighty God,
we pray that your servant _____,
who has undertaken the government of the *realm* by your mercy,
may also increase in all virtues,
and strengthened in them may avoid the enormity of sin,
and follow you, the Way, the Truth, and the Life,
and be acceptable in your sight;
through Jesus Christ our Lord. [338]

p. 103.2, Gregorian

4. For a Family.

Almighty and eternal God,
help us in our duties
and protect all who dwell in this house,
that all may know you as the Defender of your family
and the Inhabitant of this dwelling;
through Jesus Christ our Lord. [339]

p. 103.3, Gelasian

Hear us, holy Lord, Father almighty, eternal God,
and send your holy angels from heaven
to guard, cherish, protect, visit,
and defend all who dwell in this house;
through Jesus Christ our Lord. [340]

p. 104.1, Gelasian

O Lord,
unite your servants
as they seek you with all their heart,
serve you with submissive minds,
humbly implore your mercy,
and constantly rejoice in your blessings;
through Jesus Christ our Lord. [341]

p. 104.2, Gelasian

5.   *For Relations and Friends.*

O Lord,
extend your mercy
over your servants _____, _____,
with the right hand of your heavenly help,
that they may seek you with all their heart,
and obtain what they ask per your will;
through Christ our Lord. [342]

p. 104.3, Gelasian

O God,
by the grace of the Holy Spirit
you poured the gift of love
into the hearts of your faithful people.
Give your servants _____, _____,
health of body and soul
that they may love you with all their strength,
and moved by love, do what pleases you;
through Jesus Christ our Lord. [343]

p. 104.4, Gregorian

O God,
you are pleased to hear
the prayers of your people
who serve in love.
Grant that your servants _____, _____,
may grow in your love
and rejoice in your protection
that they may serve you with a quiet mind
and always remain in your peace;
through Jesus Christ our Lord. [344]

p. 105.1, Gregorian

Almighty and eternal God,
have mercy on your servant _____,
and guide *him* by your grace
in the way of eternal salvation,
that *he* may desire what pleases you,
and with all power may perform it;
through our Lord. [345]

p. 105.2, Gregorian

O Christ,
my Creator and Redeemer,
almighty Lord God,
forgive the sins of all
who are joined to me by friendship or blood,
and for whom I pray, or have resolved to pray, —
and all your faithful people.
Deliver them from all evil,
preserve them in all good,
and bring them to eternal joy. [346]

p. 105.3, Corbey Manuscript / Gregorian

Most high God,
our loving Father,
you are infinite in majesty.
I humbly pray for your servant _____.
Give *him* a pure mind, perfect love,
sincerity in conduct, purity in heart,
strength in action, courage in distress
self-control in character.
Hear *his* prayers and bless *him*.
Protect *him* under the shadow of your wings,
and hear my prayers for *him* in your mercy.
Pardon *his* sins, perfect *his* work, accept *his* prayers.
Protect *him* by your name, O God of Jacob!
Send *him* your saving help from your holy place,
and strengthen *him* out of Zion.
Receive *his* offerings, accept *his* sacrifice,
give *him* the grace of devotion,
fulfil *his* desire with good gifts,
and crown *him* with mercy.
As *he* serves you with faithful devotion,
pardon *his* sins,
correct *him* with Fatherly tenderness,
and direct *him* on your righteous path.
Deliver *him* from all troubles,
that declared righteous by you,
both here and eternally,

he may praise you forever with the angels,
saying, "Holy, Holy, Holy." [347]

p. 105.4, Gallican

Give those we love,
or those related to us,
or those who share our faith
full devotion to you.
Fill them with the Spirit of your love,
cleanse them from earthly desires,
and by your grace,
give them heavenly blessedness. [348]

p. 106.1, Gallican, 10th C.

6.   *For a Friend before a Journey.*

O God,
you always have mercy on those who love you,
and you are near those who serve you.
Direct your servant _____ with your will,
protect and guide *him* in the paths of righteousness;
through Jesus Christ our Lord. [349]

p. 107.1, Gelasian

O Lord, hear our prayers,
and accompany your servant _____ on *his* journey.
Since you are everywhere,
bless *him* with your mercy everywhere.
Help and defend *him* in all trouble
that *he* may enjoy the fulfilment
of *his* prayers in your name;
through Jesus Christ our Lord. [350]

p. 107.2, Gelasian

God of infinite mercy
and boundless majesty,
no distance of place or length of time
can separate you from those you love.
Be with your servants who confide in you.
Wherever they go,
be their Guide and Companion.
Let no trouble harm them
and no difficulty oppose them.
Give them happiness and prosperity.
With your powerful help,
quickly grant whatever they ask in prayer
according to your will;
through Jesus Christ our Lord. [351]

p. 107.3, Gelasian

7.   For a Friend in any Danger.

O God,
you justify the ungodly,
and you do not desire the death of a sinner.
Graciously protect and help your servant _____,
who relies on your mercy,
and keep *him* safe in your protection
that *he* may continually serve you
and not be separated from you by any temptation;
through our Lord Jesus Christ. [352]

p. 108.1, Gregorian

8.   For a Friend on His Birthday.

Almighty and eternal God,
Maker of all creation,
mercifully hear our prayers,
and grant many and happy years to your servant _____,
whom you have protected from birth,
and dealt with according to your mercy,
that *he* may spend all *his* life in ways that please you;
through Jesus Christ our Lord. [353]

p. 108.2, Gelasian

O God,
you are the Life of the faithful
and the Savior and Guardian of those who fear you.
After another year,
you have brought your servant_____
to this, *his* natural birthday.
Protector of life, increase *his* time of grace
with many happy years.
When *he* has been carried through this life,
bring *him* to the height of heavenly joys;
through Jesus Christ our Lord. [354]

p. 109.1, Gelasian

9.   For the Sick.

O God,
you always govern your creatures
with tender affection.
Hear our prayers for your servant,
who is suffering from bodily sickness.
Visit *him* with your deliverance,
and give *him* the medicine of your heavenly grace;
through Jesus Christ our Lord. [355]

p. 109.2, Gelasian

O God,
you give humanity
the medicines that heal
and the gift of eternal life.
Give your servant strength,
that not only in *his* body,
but also in *his* soul,
he may experience your healing;
through Jesus Christ our Lord. [356]

p. 109.3, Gelasian

O God of heavenly powers,
by the power of your command
you can drive away
all sickness and all infirmity.
Show your goodness to your servant,
that *his* weakness may turn to strength,
and with *his* health restored
he may bless your holy name;
through our Lord Jesus Christ. [357]

p. 109.4, Gelasian

O God,
by your command
the moments of our life run their course.
Hear our prayers for your servants who are sick,
that our fears because of their illness
may be turned into joy at their recovery;
through Jesus Christ our Lord. [358]

p. 110.1, Gelasian

Almighty and eternal God,
you are the salvation of believers,
hear our prayer for your servants _____, _____,
for whom we pray.
Restore their health
that they may give thanks to you in your Church;
through Jesus Christ our Lord. [359]

p. 110.2, Gelasian

O God,
you added fifteen years
to the life of your servant Hezekiah.
By your power,
raise up your servant _____
from the bed of sickness to health;
through Jesus Christ our Lord. [360]

p. 110.3, Gregorian

O Lord,
look on your servant _____,
who is suffering from *his* sickness,
and refresh *his* soul with your promise,
that being instructed by your discipline,
he may quickly recover by your healing;
through Jesus Christ our Lord. [361]

p. 110.4, Gregorian

O God,
for you it is an easy thing to give life to the dead.
Restore the sick to their former health,
and let all who call on your heavenly mercy for healing
receive the remedies of earthly medicine;
through Jesus Christ our Lord. [362]

p. 111.1, Gothic

O Christ our Lord,
you are the Physician of salvation,
Look on all your faithful people who are sick,
who love to call on your name,
and give them the help of your heavenly healing.
Keep and deliver them from all sickness and infirmity. [363]

p. 111.2, Mozarabic

Almighty and eternal God,
you protect those who labor in danger and hardships.
We humbly pray,
send your holy angel
to uphold and comfort your servant _____,
who suffers distress and affliction,
that *he* may receive your help now
and experience your healing forever;
through Jesus Christ our Lord. [364]

p. 111.3, Gallican, 10th C.

O Lord,
help and heal your servant,
as you visited Peter's mother-in-law
and the centurion's servant.
Restore *him*, O Lord,
to *his* former health;
that *he* may say in the courts of your house,
"The Lord has disciplined me severely,
but he has not given me over to death,
he who is the Savior of the world."
Grant this, O Lord,
with the Father and the Holy Spirit

you live and reign, God,
throughout all ages. [365]

p. 111.4, Sarum Manual

Almighty and eternal God,
you nurture those who suffer in peril and need.
Send your holy angel to uplift and comfort your servant,
that *he* may both receive your present help,
and enjoy your eternal healing;
through Jesus Christ our Lord. [366]

p. 112.1, York Manual

Sovereign Lord, our God almighty,
save us all,
for you are the only Physician of souls and bodies.
Sanctify us all,
for you are the Healer of every disease.
Also, heal this your servant.
Raise *him* up from the bed of pain.
Show *him* your mercy and compassion.
Drive away from *him* all sickness and infirmity.
Raise *him* up by your mighty hand,
that *he* may serve you with all thankfulness,
and that we may share with *him* your wonderful goodness
and praise and glorify you,
for great and amazing are your deeds,
and you are worthy of all praise.
You pity and save,
and to you we ascribe glory,
Father, Son, and Holy Spirit,
now and forever. [367]

p. 112.2, Greek Office for the Sick

May the Lord forgive all your sins
and heal all your sicknesses
and save your life
and satisfy your desires in all things;
he lives and reigns,
One God in Trinity,
through eternal ages. [368]

p. 113.1, Menard's ed. Gregorian

O Lord, holy Father, almighty and eternal God,
hear us, and preserve your servant _____.
whom you have given life,
and whom you have redeemed
by the most precious gift
of the blood of your Son;
who lives and reigns with you and the Holy Spirit,
one God, now and forever. [369]

p. 113.2, Rheims Manuscript, Menard

God and King,
by your mercy,
pardon the sins of your servant _____.
Deliver *him* from all the bonds of the enemy
that *he* may cling to your commandments with all *his* heart,
and always love you alone with all *his* strength,
and one day be counted with your blessed ones;
through Christ our Lord. [370]

p. 113.3, Rheims Manuscript, Menard

10. For a Sick Person about to Commune.

O holy Lord, Father almighty, eternal God,
we pray to you in faith
that our *brother* _____,
who receives the most holy body and blood
of your Son, our Lord Jesus Christ,
may enjoy health in both body and soul;
through the same our Lord. [371]

p. 114.1, Pontifical, 9th C. Sarum / York

Lord Jesus Christ,
our Savior and Redeemer,
hear us when we pray to you
for our sick *brother* _____,
that your holy Eucharist
may strengthen and preserve *him*
in soul and body,
to life everlasting;
you live and reign
with the Father and the Holy Spirit,
one God, now and forever. [372]

p. 114.2, Pontifical, 12th C.

11. Litany for the Sick.

Lord, have mercy on *him.*
Christ, have mercy on *him.*
Lord, have mercy on *him.*

O Christ, hear us.
Be merciful, **spare** *him,* **O Lord.**
Be merciful, **deliver** *him,* **O Lord.**
From all evil, **O Lord, deliver** *him.*
From *his* sins, **O Lord, deliver** *him.*
From unholy thoughts, **O Lord, deliver** *him.*
From pain and anguish, **O Lord, deliver** *him.*
From the snares of the devil, **O Lord, deliver** *him.*
From the power of demons, **O Lord, deliver** *him.*
From all present trouble, **O Lord, deliver** *him.*
From eternal damnation, **O Lord, deliver** *him.*
From your righteous anger, **O Lord, deliver** *him.*
By the mystery of your holy incarnation, **O Lord, deliver** *him.*
By your advent, **O Lord, deliver** *him.*
By your nativity, **O Lord, deliver** *him.*
By your baptism, **O Lord, deliver** *him.*
By your passion and cross, **O Lord, deliver** *him.*
By your glorious resurrection, **O Lord, deliver** *him.*
By your wonderful ascension, **O Lord, deliver** *him.*
By the grace of the Holy Spirit, the Comforter, **O Lord, deliver** *him.*
In the hour of *his* departure, **O Lord, deliver** *him.*
We sinners ask you, **hear us.**
That you remove from *him* your anger, **we ask you to hear us, O Lord.**
That it may please you to give *him* fruitful and saving repentance, **we ask
    you to hear us, O Lord.**
That it may please you to give *him* a humble and contrite heart, **we ask
    you to hear us, O Lord.**
That it may please you to give *him* godly sorrow, **we ask you to hear us,
    O Lord.**
That it may please you to give *him* renewed faith, hope, and love, **we ask
    you to hear us, O Lord.**
That you would take away from *him* all murmuring and impatience, **we
    ask you to hear us, O Lord.**
That you would mercifully raise *him* up from the bed of sickness, **we ask
    you to hear us, O Lord.**
That you would restore *him* in health and safety to your holy Church, **we
    ask you to hear us, O Lord.**
That you would pardon all *his* sins, **we ask you to hear us, O Lord.**
That it may please you to give *him* your grace, **we ask you to hear us, O
    Lord.**
That it may please you to bless *him* with your righteous right hand, **we ask
    you to hear us, O Lord.**
Son of God, **we ask you to hear us, O Lord.**
Lamb of God, you take away the sins of the world,
Have mercy on us, and on *him,* **O Lord.** [373]

p. 114.3, Gallican and York Litanies for the Sick

12. *Prayers for the Dying.*

To you, O Lord,
we commend the soul of your servant _____.
As *he* dies to the world, may *he* live to you.
Whatever sins *he* has committed
in the weakness of earthly life,
clear away by your most loving and merciful forgiveness;
through Jesus Christ our Lord. [374]

p. 116.1, Gregorian

Almighty and eternal God,
Guardian of souls,
in your love you correct and discipline
those you receive as your children.
O Lord, give your healing to your servant _____,
who suffers in body from weakness,
pains, and the distress of disease.
O Lord, be gracious to *him*,
that *his* soul, in the hour of its departure from the body,
may be brought to you by the holy angels,
holy and blameless in Christ,[30]
to you who gave it;
through our Lord. [375]

p. 116.2, Gallican, 9th C.

Almighty and eternal God,
you breathed into man a soul in your likeness,
and at your bidding dust returns to dust.
Bring this soul to be with your chosen saints in your eternal home.
Gently and tenderly receive *him* as he returns
as from the land of Egypt to your Promised Land.
Send your holy angels to meet *him*,
show *him* the way of righteousness,
and open the gates of your glory. [376]

p. 117.1, York Manual / Salzburg / Sarum / Gelasian

Sovereign Lord, God almighty,
you want all people to be saved
and come to a knowledge of the truth.
You do not desire the death of sinners,
but that they turn to you and live.
Free the soul of your servant from every bond,
and free *him* from every curse.
For you are he who frees the captive,
and lifts up the crushed,

---

[30] This line was added to strengthen the reference to Colossians 1:22. Original translation had: "clear from all stains of deadly sin, unto Thee..."

and the Hope of the hopeless!
O Lord, release the soul of your servant in peace
to rest in your eternal dwelling with all your saints;
through your only Son.
With him and with your Holy and life-giving Spirit,
you are blessed now and forever. [377]

p. 117.2, Eastern Church Office for the Dying

13. *Litany for the Dying.*

God, the Father in heaven, **have mercy on the soul of your servant.**
God the Son, Redeemer of the world, **have mercy on the soul of your servant.**
God the Holy Spirit, **have mercy on the soul of your servant.**
Holy Trinity, One God, **have mercy on *his* soul.**
You are Three and One, **have mercy on *his* soul.**
God most holy, **have mercy on *his* soul.**
By your holy incarnation, **have mercy on *his* soul.**
By your holy nativity, **have mercy on *his* soul.**
By your holy circumcision, **have mercy on *his* soul.**
By your holy epiphany, **have mercy on *his* soul.**
By your holy baptism, **have mercy on *his* soul.**
By your holy passion, **have mercy on *his* soul.**
By your holy and most loving death, **have mercy on *his* soul.**
By your holy descent into hell, **have mercy on *his* soul.**
By your glorious resurrection, **have mercy on *his* soul.**
By your wonderful ascension, **have mercy on *his* soul.**
By the coming of the Holy Spirit, the Comforter, **have mercy on *his* soul.**
By the majesty of your coming, **we sinners pray you to hear us.**
To deliver the soul of your servant from the prince of darkness and the place of punishment, **we ask you to hear us, O Lord.**
To forget all *his* sins forever, **we ask you to hear us, O Lord.**
To mercifully pardon whatever guilt *he* contracted by the lies of the devil, or by *his* own sinfulness and weakness, **we ask you to hear us, O Lord.**
To forgive his sins as *he* has always hoped, **we ask you to hear us, O Lord.**
To give this our *brother,* as *he* returns to you, a place of refreshment, light, and eternal blessedness, **we ask you to hear us, O Lord.**
To give *him* joy and gladness in your kingdom, with your saints and elect, **we ask you to hear us, O Lord.**
that *he* may wait for the Day of Judgment with confidence, **we ask you to hear us, O Lord.**
To show *him* the blessed vision of your holy and glorious face looking on *him* with kindness, **we ask you to hear us, O Lord.**
To hear us, Son of God, **we ask you to hear us, O Lord.**

Lamb of God, you take away the sins of the world, **have mercy on *his* soul.**

Lamb of God, you take away the sins of the world, **give *him* peace, eternal happiness and glory.**

Lord, have mercy on *him.*

Christ, have mercy on *him.*

Lord, have mercy on *him.* [378]

p. 118.1, Litanies of Sarum, Fleury Jumièges, Rouen

14. *A Final Commendation of the Dying.*

Depart, Christian soul, out of this world,
in the name of God the Father almighty who created you,
in the name of Jesus Christ his Son, who suffered for you,
in the name of the Holy Spirit, who has been poured out into you.
May you depart this day in peace,
and your home be in the heavenly Jerusalem. [379]

p. 120.1, Commendation in Sarum

15. *For the Afflicted.*

Grant your mercy, relief and refreshment to every Christian soul that is afflicted, or distressed. [380]

p. 121.1, Liturgy of St. Mark

O Lord,
do not despise those who cry out in their afflictions,
but mercifully relieve their pain and help them quickly;
through Jesus Christ our Lord. [381]

p. 121.2, Leonine

Almighty and eternal God,
the Comfort of the sad,
the Strength of sufferers,
hear the prayers of those who call to you in any trouble,
that they may rejoice to know
your mercy is with them in their afflictions;
through Christ our Lord. [382]

p. 121.3, Gelasian, Good Friday

O Lord,
give strength to the weary,
help to the sufferers,
comfort for the sad,
help to those in trouble. [383]

p. 121.4, Ambrosian

Look on and relieve
the miseries of the poor and captives.
We pray, hear us. [384]

p. 121.5, Sarum Litany

O Lord,
your mercy is great
in relieving the captives,
sparing the wretched,
forgiving sinners,
supporting travelers,
comforting the oppressed,
hearing prayers,
giving the poor what they need,
and converting heathen nations to call on your name.
O loving and merciful God,
hear us when we ask for mercy. [385]

p. 121.6, Gallican Sacramentary

O God,
you are the Author of love,
and you love pure peace and affection.
Heal the diseases of all Christians who are sick,
and in your great mercy set free
all who are terrified by fears,
afflicted by poverty,
weary with trouble,
worn down by illness,
burdened with punishment,
and all prisoners and wanderers.
Show them your compassion daily.
Tenderly lift them up, correct them,
and protect them. [386]

p. 122.1, Gallican Sacramentary

O God,
our Refuge in pains,
our Strength in weakness,
our Help in trouble,
our Comfort in tears.
O Lord, spare your people.
Do not forsake the souls who praise you.[31] [387]

p. 122.2, Gallican Sacramentary

16. For all in Error or Sin.

O God of heavenly powers,
fulfil your promised mercy,
that the hearts of the rebellious
may be subdued to the truth of the Gospel;
through Jesus Christ our Lord. [388]

p. 122.3, Leonine

---

[31] Original translation: "spare Thy people, give not up to beasts the souls that praise Thee." The last line in the original is a reference to Ps. 74:19

Almighty and eternal God,
you save all, and are not willing that any should perish.
Look on those who have been deceived by the lies of the devil,
that all false teachings may be driven away
and the hearts of those who have gone astray may repent
and return to your unshaken truth;
through Jesus Christ our Lord. [389]

p. 123.1, Gelasian, Good Friday

O Christ,
dissolve the divisions of heresy
which try overturn the faith and corrupt the truth.
Since you are acknowledged in heaven and in earth
as one and the same Lord,
let your people, gathered from all nations
serve you in unity of faith. [390]

p. 123.2, Mozarabic

O Lord,
have mercy on those who have forgotten their baptism,[32]
that they may again be adorned with the gifts of faithful repentance;
through Jesus Christ our Lord. [391]

p. 123.3, Gallican

Most merciful God,
you recall those who have gone astray
and do not despise sinners.
We rely on your promise, O Lord,
that you will pardon those who repent.
May all who seek you find you. [392]

p. 123.4, Gallican Sacramentary

O Lord,
have mercy on your servants—
put away all their wickedness
and protect them by your compassion,
that they may increase
in the keeping of your commandments,
that in this life they may avoid all sins,
and one day come to your glory
without confusion. [393]

p. 124.1, Gallican Sacramentary

That you would bring back the straying to the way of salvation:
We pray you, hear us. [394]

p. 124.2, Lyons Litany

---

[32] Original translation: "Grant, O Lord, to those who have lost the grace of the font, ..."

O God,
you delight in the devotion of the faithful.
Make your people devoted to your holy things.
If some depart from their duties
by ungodly thoughts or actions,
convert them by your grace
and free them from the snares of the devil;
through Jesus Christ our Lord. [395]

17. For Jews and Heathen.

Almighty and eternal God,
you do not exclude any from your mercy.[33]
Hear the prayers we offer for your ancient people,
that acknowledging Jesus Christ
as the Light of truth
they may be delivered from their darkness;
through the same Jesus Christ our Lord. [396]

p. 124.4, Gelasian, Good Friday

Almighty and eternal God,
you do not desire the death of sinners,
but that they return to you and live.
In mercy, hear our prayer.
Deliver the heathen from idolatry,
and gather them into your holy Church
to the praise and glory of your name;
through Jesus Christ our Lord. [397]

p. 125.1, Gelasian

O God,
grant that all the inhabitants of the world
may become children of Abraham
and have the dignity of true Israelites;
through Jesus Christ our Lord. [398]

p. 125.2, Gelasian

O Lord, holy Father, eternal God,
command the way of your truth
and of the knowledge of you
to be shown to your servants
who wander in doubt and uncertainty
in the darkness of this world.
Open the eyes of their souls,
that they may acknowledge you,

---

[33] Original translation, instead of "any," "even the faithless Jews." And instead of "your ancient people," "that blinded people."

97

the One God,
the Father in the Son, and the Son in the Father,
with the Holy Spirit,
and enjoy the fruit of this confession
both here and in the world to come;
through Jesus Christ our Lord. [399]

p. 125.3, Gregorian

O God,
you are rich in mercy to all.
Father of glory,
you gave your Son to be a light to the Gentiles,
to proclaim freedom to the captives
and sight to the blind.
In Christ you are boundless in compassion.
Forgive their sins,
and through faith give them a portion among the saints. [400]

p. 126.1, Gallican Sacramentary

Almighty Lord our God,
guide our feet into the way of peace,
and strengthen our hearts to obey your commands.
May the sunrise dawn upon us
and give light to those who sit in darkness
and in the shadow of death,
that they may adore you for your mercy,
follow you for your truth,
and desire you for your sweetness,
for you are the blessed Lord God of Israel. [401]

p. 126.2, *Collectio post Prophetiam*, after the Benedictus

18. General Pleading.

We sinners ask you, **hear us.**

To defend and exalt your Church, **we ask you, Lord Jesus, to hear us.**

To grant to your Church the tranquility of peace, **we ask you, Lord Jesus, to hear us.**

to defeat the enemies of God's holy Church, **we ask you, Lord Jesus, to hear us.**

to defend us from dangerous enemies, **we ask you, Lord Jesus, to hear us.**

to preserve _____, our pastor and chief priest, and the flock committed to him, **we ask you, Lord Jesus, to hear us.**

to always keep the *Queen* in prosperity, **we ask you, Lord Jesus, to hear us.**

to preserve all orders of the Church, the clergy and laity, and all the people of God, **we ask you, Lord Jesus, to hear us.**

to make us persevere in good works, **we ask you, Lord Jesus, to hear us.**

to give us heavenly armor against the devil, **we ask you, Lord Jesus, to hear us.**

that your mercy and pity may keep us safe, **we ask you, Lord Jesus, to hear us.**

that you would give us the will and the power to repent, **we ask you, Lord Jesus, to hear us.**

to pardon all our sins, **we ask you, Lord Jesus, to hear us.**

to give us right faith, firm hope in your goodness, perfect love, and constant fear of you, **we ask you, Lord Jesus, to hear us.**

to remove evil thoughts from us, **we ask you, Lord Jesus, to hear us.**

to pour into our souls the grace of the Holy Spirit, **we ask you, Lord Jesus, to hear us.**

to give us constant light, **we ask you, Lord Jesus, to hear us.**

to give us a happy end, **we ask you, Lord Jesus, to hear us.**

to bring us to eternal joys, **we ask you, Lord Jesus, to hear us.**

Son of God, **hear us.**

Lamb of God, you away the sins of the world, **spare us.**

Lamb of God, you away the sins of the world, **give us pardon.**

Lamb of God, you away the sins of the world, **hear us.** [402]

p. 126.3, Gallican Litanies

Give completeness to beginners,
understanding to the little ones,
and help to those who are running their course.
Give sorrow to the negligent,
fervor to the lukewarm,
and to the mature a true humility. [403]

p. 128.1, Gallican Litanies

99

PRAYERS BEFORE CHURCH SERVICE

O life-giving Master and Bestower of good things,
you have given us the blessed hope of eternal life,
our Lord Jesus Christ.
May we perform this divine service to you in holiness,
that we may enjoy the blessedness to come,
and guarded by your power,
and guided into the light of truth
always give you all glory and thanksgiving. [404]

p. 129.1, Liturgy of St. James

Holy, Most High, Awesome,
you dwell in the holy place.
Make us holy,
bring us near to you and cleanse us from all sin
that we may perform worship in your fear,
for you bless and hallow all things. [405]

p. 129.2, Liturgy of St. Mark

Lord,
God of inconceivable power,
incomprehensible glory,
immeasurable mercy,
unspeakable kindness,
look on us in your tender love
and show your rich mercy and compassion
to us and those who pray with us. [406]

p. 129.3, Liturgy of St. Chrysostom

O gracious King of ages,
Master of all creation,
receive your Church that approaches you through Christ.
Give each of us what is good,
bring us all to completeness
and make us ready by your sanctifying grace.
Unite us together in your Holy Church,
which you purchased with the precious blood of your only Son,
our Lord and Savior Jesus Christ;
with him, and with your all-holy, good, and life-giving Spirit,
you are blessed and glorified forever. [407]

p. 130.1, Liturgy of St. James

PRAYERS AFTER CHURCH SERVICE

O God,
you have spoken
your divine and saving Word into our ears.
Enlighten the souls of us sinners
to fully understand
what has been spoken,
that we may not be mere hearers of spiritual words
but also doers of good works,
following with sincere faith,
blameless life,
and good conduct;
through Jesus Christ our Lord. [408]

p. 131.1, Liturgy of St. James

Lord and Master,
Jesus Christ,
Co-eternal Word of the Father,
to save us, you became like us in every way, except without sin,
Move us not only to be hearers of the Word
but also doers,
and to bring forth good fruit,
thirty, sixty or a hundred times what was sown,
and be received into the kingdom of heaven.
Let your love overtake our hearts,
for the gospel proclaims you,
O Savior and Guardian of our souls and bodies,
and to you we ascribe all glory. [409]

p. 131.2, Liturgy of St. Mark

O Lord God,
you taught us to pray together
and have promised to hear
even two or three calling on your name.
Lord, hear the prayers of your servants.
Give us knowledge of your truth and salvation,
and in the world to come,
give us life eternal. [410]

p. 131.3, Armenian Liturgy

O Lord,
hear the humble prayers of your family,
that by your help
they may persevere
in the confession of your name;
through Jesus Christ our Lord. [411]

p. 132.1, Leonine

O Lord,
have pity on our earnest prayers.
Since we can claim nothing by our merits
answer and give by the abundance of your pardon;
through Jesus Christ our Lord. [412]

p. 132.2, Leonine

O God of heavenly powers,
you give more than we ask or deserve.
Since we cannot rely on ourselves and deserve nothing,
grant our prayers by your mercy;
through Jesus Christ our Lord. [413]

p. 132.3, Leonine / Gelasian, Trinity 12

O Lord,
continue to give your gifts to your faithful servants,
that in receiving them we may seek you,
and in seeking you we may continue to receive them;
through Jesus Christ our Lord. [414]

p. 132.4, Gelasian

O Lord,
bless your family in heavenly places,[34]
and fill them with your spiritual gifts.
Give them love, joy, peace,
patience, goodness, gentleness,
hope, faith, purity,
that being refreshed by all your gifts,
they may receive what they desire
and come safe to you;
through our Lord. [415]

p. 133.1, Gelasian

Lord,
open your heavens,
open our eyes.
From there your gifts descend to us,
from here may our hearts look back to you.
May your throne be open to us

---

[34] Ephesians 1:3.

as we receive the benefits we ask.
May our minds be open to you
while we serve as you have commanded us.
Look down from heaven, O Lord.
Visit and tend this vine you have planted.
Strengthen the weak,
relieve the contrite,
confirm the strong.
Build them up in love,
cleanse them with purity,
enlighten them with wisdom,
keep them with mercy.
Lord Jesus, Good Shepherd,
you laid down your life for the sheep.
Defend those you purchased with your blood.
Feed the hungry,
give drink to the thirsty,
seek the lost,
call back the wandering,
heal what is broken.
Stretch forth your hand from heaven
and touch the head of each one.
May they feel the touch of your hand
and receive the joy of the Holy Spirit,
that they may remain blessed forevermore. [416]

p. 133.2, Benedictionale of St. Ethelwold

EUCHARISTIC PRAYERS

1. Before the Celebration

O Lord,
take away all our iniquities,
and the spirit of pride and arrogance which you resist.
Fill us with the spirit of fear,
and give us humble and contrite hearts which you do not despise,
that we may enter the Holy of Holies with pure minds;
through Jesus Christ our Lord. [417]

p. 135.1, Mozarabic / Leonine

O God the Father,
in your great and wonderful love to us
you sent your Son into the world
to bring back the wandering sheep.
Do not turn your face away from us
when we approach your altar.[35]
We do not trust our righteousness,
but your gracious compassion and redemption. [418]

p. 135.2, Liturgy of St. James

O Lord God our Master,
do not reject me,
although I am defiled by many sins.
See, I approach your divine and heavenly sacrament,[36]
not because I am worthy,
but looking only to your goodness.
I lift up my voice to you.
O God, be merciful to me a sinner.
I have sinned against heaven and against you,
and am not worthy to look on this, your holy and spiritual table,
where your only Son our Lord Jesus Christ
offers himself to me, a sinner,[37]
one stained with every defilement. [419]

p. 135.3, Liturgy of St. James

O Lord our God,
Bread of heaven,
Life of the world,
I have sinned against heaven and against you,
and am not worthy to partake of your holy sacrament,

---

[35] Original translation: "when we approach this Thy tremendous and unbloody sacrifice."
[36] Original translation: "Mystery." Sacrament (Latin) is a word often used to translate the Greek word *mysterion*. For clarity and consistency, I have preferred the word "sacrament" in the revision of these Eucharistic prayers.
[37] Original translation: "is mystically set forth as a sacrifice for me a sinner."

but in your divine tenderness you give your grace
to partake of your holy body and precious blood,
without condemnation, for forgiveness of sins and eternal life. [420]

p. 136.1, Liturgy of St. James

O Lord our God,
you have called us Christians
after the name of your only Son,
and have given us baptism in the font
for the forgiveness of sins.
Receive us now to this communion[38]
for the forgiveness of our sins,
that we may glorify you with thanksgiving. [421]

p. 136.2, Armenian Liturgy

O Lord my God,
let me receive the body and blood of your Son,
our Lord Jesus Christ,
that by it I may receive forgiveness of all my sins,
and be filled with your Holy Spirit;
O our God, you live and reign forever and ever. [422]

p. 136.3, Mozarabic

Cleanse us, O Lord, from our secret faults,
and mercifully forgive our presumptuous sins,
that we may receive your holy things with a pure mind;
through Jesus Christ our Lord. [423]

p. 137.1, Leonine

O Lord,
grant that our bodies may be sanctified by your holy body,
and our souls purified by your atoning blood,
that they may give us pardon of our offences
and forgiveness of our sins.
Glory be to you forever, O Lord God. [424]

p. 137.2, Syrian Liturgy of St. James

Lord, I am not worthy that you should come under my roof,
but relying on your loving-kindness
I draw near your altar:
sick, to the Physician of life,
blind, to the Light of eternal brightness,
poor, to the Lord of heaven and earth,
naked, to the King of glory,
a sheep, to its Shepherd,
a creature, to its Creator,
desolate, to the loving Comforter,

---

[38] Original translation: "make us, we beseech Thee, worthy now to receive this Communion"

miserable, to the Merciful,
a criminal, to the Giver of pardon,
ungodly, to the Justifier,
hardened, to the Giver of grace, [39]
relying on your overflowing and infinite mercy,
to heal my weakness,
wash my foulness, enlighten my blindness,
enrich my poverty, clothe my nakedness,
bring me back from my wanderings,
console my sadness, forgive my guiltiness,
give pardon to the sinner, forgiveness to the miserable,
life to the criminal, justification to the dead,
that I may receive you,
Bread of angels, King of kings, and Lord of lords,
with such chastity of body and purity of mind,
such contrition of heart and plenteous sorrow,
such spiritual gladness and heavenly joy,
such fear and trembling, such reverence and honor,
such faith and humility, such purpose and love,
such devotion and thanksgiving, as are good and right,
that it profits me to life eternal and for the forgiveness of all my sins. [425]

p. 137.3, Sarum / Thomas Aquinas

O God the Father in heaven, **have mercy on us.**
O God the Son, Redeemer of the world, **have mercy on us.**
O God the Holy Spirit, **have mercy on us.**
Holy Trinity, One God, **have mercy on us.**
Help us, O God our Savior, **have mercy on us.**
From the dominion of all vices, **O Lord deliver us.**
From blindness of heart, **O Lord deliver us.**
From all evil, **O Lord deliver us.**
We sinners, **ask you to hear us.**
That you would spare us, **we ask you to hear us.**
That you would give us a sure hope, **we ask you to hear us.**
That you would give us a right faith, **we ask you to hear us.**
That you would give us perfect love, **we ask you to hear us.**
That you would mortify in us all vices, **we ask you to hear us.**
That you would awaken us with your virtues, **we ask you to hear us.**
That by your incarnation you would open for us the Holy of Holies, **we ask you to hear us.**
That by this most holy mystery you would renew our souls and bodies, **we ask you to hear us.**
That we may handle with pure hands this wonderful sacrament, **we ask you to hear us.**

---

[39] Original translation: Instead of "giver" it had "Infuser."

That we may receive it with pure minds, **we ask you to hear us.**
That by it we receive pardon for all sins, **we ask you to hear us.**
That by it we may always cling to you, **we ask you to hear us.**
That by it we may have you dwelling in us, and ourselves dwelling in you,
    we ask you to hear us.
That by it you pour into our hearts the grace of the Holy Spirit, **we ask**
    you to hear us.
That you preserve the Christian people who have been redeemed by your
    precious blood, **we ask you to hear us.**
That you give us a place of repentance, **we ask you to hear us.** [426]

p. 138.1, Litany, 10th C. Manuscript

2. *At the Offertory.*

We give you thanks,
O Lord God, Father almighty,
together with your Son, our Lord God and Savior Jesus Christ
and the Holy Spirit,
and we offer to you our prayer and praise [40]
which all nations offer to you, O Lord,
from the rising of the sun to its setting,
from the north and from the south,
for great is your name in all nations,
and everywhere incense and offerings
are given to your holy name. [427]

p. 140.1, Liturgy of St. Mark

O Lord, receive the offerings of our worship
and by the glorious sacrament[41]
purify the hearts of those that are subject to you. [428]

p. 140.2, Leonine

O Lord, send the Holy Spirit,
and by your sacrament to us,
purify our hearts by its reception.[42] [429]

p. 140.3, Leonine

O Lord,
in your mercy bless these gifts,
receive our offerings,
and make us living sacrifices to you;[43]
through Jesus Christ our Lord. [430]

p. 141.1, Leonine

---

[40] Original translation: "this reasonable and unbloody service" and later, "incense and sacrifice and oblation are offered unto Thy holy Name."

[41] Original translation: instead of "sacrament," "oblation"

[42] Original translation: "...Spirit, to make these present offerings Thy sacrament unto us, and purify...."

[43] Original translation: "and having received the offering of the spiritual sacrifice, to make us a perpetual oblation unto Thee;" Revision sharpens the reference to Romans 12:1.

O Lord, look mercifully on these offerings we present,
that they may display our devotion for your salvation;[44]
through Jesus Christ our Lord. [431]

p. 141.2, Leonine

3. For the other Communicants.

O Lord, remember your servants here, whose faith and devotion are
discerned and known by you. [432]

p. 141.3, Roman Canon / Gelasian

4. For a Friend.

O Lord, have mercy on your servant _____,
for whom I offer my prayers to your majesty,[45]
that he may lead a good life in this world,
and happily receive eternal blessedness. [433]

p. 141.4, from two Gregorian prayers

O Lord, receive the prayers[46]
I humbly offer to your majesty
for the welfare of your servant _____,
that his life, in good times and bad
may always be guided by your providence;
through Jesus Christ our Lord. [434]

p. 141.5, Gregorian

5. Before the Consecration.

Christ, our Lord and God,
of his own free will
was made like mortals throughout his life,
showed you a body undefiled,
and atoning for the ancient offence,
exhibited a soul pure and untouched by sins,
and also commanded
that whenever we eat the bread and drink the cup,
we proclaim his death until he comes.[47]
We now remember the passion
and proclaim the eternal glory
of Jesus Christ your Son, our Lord and God,
and pray you to bless this sacrament,
and pour out your Holy Spirit,
on all who receive it;[48]
through Jesus Christ your Son, our Lord and God. [435]

p. 142.1, Ancient Missal, Gallican or Gothic

---

[44] Original translation: "avail both for our devotion and our salvation"
[45] Original translation: "for whom I offer this sacrifice of praise to Thy Majesty;"
[46] Original translation: "May the oblation, O Lord, be of good effect, which I humbly offer..."
[47] "that whenever... until he comes," Original translation: "That as often as His body and His blood
should be received, a Commemoration should be made of the Lord's Passion,"
[48] Original translation adds: "that it may be to all who receive it a pure, true, and legitimate Eucharist;"

Jesus, Good High Priest,
be present with us,
as you were when surrounded by your disciples.[49] [436]

p. 142.2, Mozarabic

6. After the Consecration.

This is truly and indeed the body and blood
of Emmanuel our God. [437]

p. 143.1, Coptic Liturgy of St. Basil

Holy things for holy people.
There is one holy, one Lord Jesus Christ,
to the glory of God the Father,
to whom be glory forever and ever.
You came into the world to save sinners
of whom I am the chief.
I confess to you like the repentant thief,
"Remember me, Lord, in your kingdom." [438]

p. 143.2, Liturgy of St. Chrysosotom

O true Father,
look at your Son,
who gave the sacrifice pleasing to you.
Through him who died for me, be merciful to me.
Look on the blood shed by wicked men on Golgotha, which pleads for me.
Accept my prayers for Christ's sake.
My offences are not greater than your compassion.
Your goodness outweighs the hills
if you would weigh them in a balance.
Do not look at my sins,
but at Christ's sacrifice for them,
for that sacrifice covers my guilt.[50]
Because of the sins I have committed,
your beloved One endured the nails and spear.
His sufferings have appeased you,
and are the means of life to me.
Glory be to the Father who gave up his Son for our salvation,
and to the Son who died on the cross, and bestowed life on us all,
and to the Spirit who began and finished the mystery of our salvation.
O most high Trinity, spare us all! [439]

p. 143.3, Common Order of the Syriac Liturgy

---

[49] Original translation continued: "Sanctify this oblation."
[50] Original translation: "Behold my sins, but behold also the sacrifice presented for them; for that sacrifice is much greater than my guilt."

We are guilty, O Father almighty,
because of our frequent sins,
guilty because of the neglect of your graces.
But the sacrifice of your only Son,
offered up to you with his blood,
has cleansed our guilty conscience
from these trespasses.
May it also be our help
when we offend after being redeemed,
since it bestows the grace of repentance
on those who do not sin against the Spirit
even until the Last Day.
So may Christ our Lord and eternal Redeemer,
our Advocate with the Father,
plead for the forgiveness of our iniquities.
Reconcile sinners by the blood of the Righteous One.
Acknowledge the Victim
by whose intervention you have been appeased,
and receive us as your adopted children
since you have become our Father through grace. [440]

p. 144.1, from two Mozarabic prayers

O taste and see that the Lord is good! Alleluia!
Praise the Lord from the heavens! Alleluia!
Praise him in the heights! Alleluia!
Praise him, all his angels! Alleluia!
Praise him, all his hosts! Alleluia!
What blessing or thanksgiving can we offer for this sacrament?
You alone, O Jesus, do we bless,
with the Father and the most Holy Spirit, now and forever. [441]

p. 145.1, Armenian

Christ gives the bread of the saints
and the cup of life for forgiveness of sins.
You are Christ our Lord and Savior,
who was born of the virgin Mary.
While we receive this most holy cup,
deliver us forever from all sin. [442]

p. 145.2, Ambrosian

O Lord, we your servants
bow before your holy altar,
awaiting your rich mercies.
O Lord, send your abundant grace and blessing,
and hallow our souls and bodies and spirits,
that we may be worthy communicants

of your holy sacrament of forgiveness of sins
and eternal life. [443]

p. 145.3, Liturgy of St. James

To you we commend our whole life and hope,
O Lord, the Lover of humanity,
and pray that we may partake
of your heavenly and awesome sacrament
from this holy and spiritual table
with a pure conscience,
for the forgiveness of sins,
and pardon of transgressions,
and communion of the Holy Spirit,
and inheritance in the kingdom of heaven,
and confidence toward you,
and not in judgment or condemnation. [444]

p. 146.1, Liturgy of St. Chrysostom

O Lord Jesus Christ,
grant that the sacrament of your body and blood,
which I receive, though undeserving,
may not be for my judgment and condemnation,
but a blessing through your loving-kindness
to the salvation of my body and soul. [445]

p. 146.2, Sarum

May your spotless body be the means of my life,
and your holy blood be the cleansing and forgiveness of my sins. [446]

p. 146.3, Armenian

7.   *After Communicating.*

O God,
in your deep and wonderful love for humanity
you reached down to help us in our weakness,
and made us partakers of this heavenly table.
Do not condemn us sinners
after the reception of your holy sacrament,
but guard us, in your goodness,
in the sanctification of the Holy Spirit,
that being made holy
we may find our portion and inheritance
with all your saints[51]
in the light of your presence;
through the mercies of your only Son
our Lord God and Savior Jesus Christ. [447]

p. 146.4, Liturgy of St. James

---

51 Original translation adds: "...Saints who have pleased Thee from the beginning, in the light..."

You have sanctified us, O Lord,
by the communion
of the most holy body and precious blood of your only Son.
Grant us the grace and gift of your Holy Spirit.
Keep us blameless in life,
and lead us on to perfect adoption and redemption
and the eternal joys to come. [448]

p. 147.1, Liturgy of St. James

We thank you, loving Master,
Benefactor of our souls,
for having admitted us
to your heavenly and immortal mysteries.
Guide us in your right path,
establish us in your fear,
watch over our lives,
make safe our goings. [449]

p. 147.2, Liturgy of St. Chrysostom

We give you thanks, O Lord our God,
for giving us your holy, spotless,
immortal, and heavenly sacrament
for the benefit, sanctification,
and healing of our souls and bodies.
O good Lord, the Lover of all,
grant that the communion
of the holy body and precious blood
of your only Son
may preserve us in faith
that does not need to be ashamed:
love with sincerity,
fullness of wisdom,
healing of soul and body,
repulse of every enemy,
fulfilment of your commandments,
an acceptable defense
before the awesome judgment-seat of your Christ. [450]

p. 147.3, Liturgy of St. Basil

What blessing,
what praise,
what thanksgiving
can we give you, O God, lover of all?
For when we were in the darkness of death
and drowning in the depths of sin
you granted us freedom
and gave us this immortal and heavenly food,

112

and revealed to us the mystery kept hidden for ages and generations.
Help us understand your supreme mercy,
and the greatness of your goodness,
and your Fatherly care for us. [451]

p. 148.1, Coptic Liturgy of St. Cyril

Lead us not into temptation,
since we have partaken
of the holy body and precious blood.
We thank you
that you have received us as communicants
of the sacrament of glory and holiness
which passes all understanding. [452]

p. 148.2, Ethiopic

Lord Jesus Christ,
you have fed us with your goodness
for salvation and life eternal.
Preserve us by this food
in purity and without defilement,
dwelling within us by your divine protection.
Guide us on the path of your holy will
by your divine grace which desires our good,
and by it may we be strengthened
against all the assaults of our enemies,
that we may hear your voice and follow you,
our mighty and true Shepherd,
and inherit the place prepared in your heavenly kingdom,
O our God and Savior Jesus Christ. [453]

p. 148.3, Armenian

Light from Light, and God from God,
you came down from your holy heavens,
and descended to earth for the salvation of the world
out of your love of humanity.
Stretch forth your almighty right hand
and send your blessings on us all.
Hallow our bodies and souls by this sacrament
and guide our steps on the path of righteousness
that we may live according to your will,
observe your commandments all the days of our lives,
come to a blessed end,
and with your saints, sing unending praises to you,
and your Father, and your Holy Spirit. [454]

p. 149.1, Liturgy of Dioscorus

Grant, O Lord,
that what we have taken with our mouth
we may receive with our soul,
and let what has been a temporary gift
become our eternal remedy;
through Jesus Christ our Lord. [455]

p. 149.2, Leonine

O Lord,
pour on us the Spirit of your love,
that those you have satisfied with heavenly bread
you may preserve in devotion. [456]

p. 150.1, Leonine, Easter

We have received life and refreshment
through the most holy body and blood of our Lord Jesus Christ.
O God, by this transcendent remedy
cleanse us from the corruption of all sins,
and strengthen us against the attack of any danger;
through the same Jesus Christ our Lord. [457]

p. 150.2, Leonine

We give thanks and praise to you, O Lord,
that you have strengthened us
with the communion of the body and blood
of your beloved Son.
May this your sacrament, O Lord,
not increase our guilt and punishment,
but plead for our pardon and salvation.
May it abolish our sins,
strengthen our weakness,
and be our never-failing bulwark against the perils of the world.
May this communion cleanse us from guilt
and make us partakers of the joy of heaven;
through Jesus Christ our Lord. [458]

p. 150.2, Leonine

May the sacred Feast of your table, O Lord,
always strengthen and renew us,
guide and protect us in our weakness
through the storms of this world,
and bring us into the harbor of eternal salvation;
through Jesus Christ our Lord. [459]

p. 151.1, Leonine

O Lord, visit your family,
and guard the hearts
which have been hallowed by this holy sacrament,
that as we receive the healing gifts of eternal salvation,

we may retain them by your protecting power;
through Jesus Christ our Lord. [460]

p. 151.2, Leonine

O Lord,
protect those you have satisfied with heavenly gifts.
Set us free from all hurtful things
that we may press onwards with our whole heart
to the salvation which comes from you;
through Jesus Christ our Lord. [461]

p. 151.3, Leonine

O Lord,
we have received your glorious sacrament.
By this, make us partakers of heavenly things
while we are dwelling here on earth;
through Jesus Christ our Lord. [462]

p. 151.4 Leonine

O Lord,
since we received your sacrament,
cleanse us from all our old sins
and change us into new creatures;
through Jesus Christ our Lord. [463]

p. 151.5, Leonine

O Lord our God,
you have filled us with restoration and life.
Help us cling to heavenly things
by the gifts you bestow on us;
through Jesus Christ our Lord. [464]

p. 152.1, Leonine

O Lord our God,
you have refreshed us
with the participation in your sacred gift.
May we also experience its work and effect;
through the same Jesus Christ our Lord. [465]

p. 152.2, Leonine

O Lord, hear our prayers,
that the Holy Communion of our redemption
may help us in this life,
and bring us to eternal joys;
through Jesus Christ our Lord. [466]

p. 152.3, Leonine

O Lord,
you have strengthened us with the gift of our redemption.
May it always help us in true faith for our eternal salvation;
through Jesus Christ our Lord. [467]

p. 152.4, Leonine

May the holy food and drink benefit us, O Lord.
May it strengthen us in our earthly life, and give us life eternal;
through Jesus Christ our Lord. [468]

p. 152.5, Leonine

O God,
you touch us when we participate in your sacrament.
Work its power in our hearts,
that through your gift we also worthily receive it;
through Jesus Christ our Lord. [469]

p. 153.1, Leonine

O Lord,
may this heavenly sacrament renew us in soul and body.
As we have received it, may we enjoy its blessing;
through Jesus Christ our Lord. [470]

p. 153.2, Leonine

O Lord,
we thank you,
for you refresh us both
with the partaking of the heavenly sacrament
and with the remembrance of your righteous servants;
through Jesus Christ our Lord. [471]

p. 153.3, Leonine, for a saint's day

May your table, O God,
set us free from earthly delights,
and always supply us with heavenly food;
through Jesus Christ our Lord. [472]

p. 153.4, Leonine

May the vices of our hearts be overcome by this medicine,
which was given to heal the diseases of our mortal nature. [473]

p. 153.5, Leonine

Almighty and eternal God,
preserve the works of your mercy,
and pour into our hearts
the sweetness of the body and blood of your only Son
Jesus Christ our Lord. [474]

p. 153.6, Leonine

O Lord, may the sharing of your sacrament
both purify us and make us one;
through Jesus Christ our Lord. [475]

p. 154.1, Gelasian

Deliver us from evil, Lord Jesus Christ!
We eat your body crucified for us,
and we drink your blood poured out for us.
May your holy body assure us of our salvation,
and your holy blood assure us of the forgiveness our sins
now and forever. [476]

p. 154.2, Gelasian

You have fed us with heavenly food,
and refreshed us with the eternal cup.
We give unceasing thanks and praise to the Lord our God.
By the most holy body of our Lord Jesus Christ,
we are freed from fleshly vices and have been made spiritual. [477]

p. 154.3, Gothic

O God,
you are eternal salvation and priceless blessedness.
Enable all your servants who have received holy and blessed things
to be holy and blessed forevermore. [478]

p. 154.4, Gothic

O God of righteousness,
God of mercy,
God of immortality and life,
God of brightness and glory,
you have refreshed us by your divine gifts.
Preserve us for yourself for the bliss to come;
through Jesus Christ our Lord. [479]

p. 155.1, Gothic

Look on us, O Lord.
You invite us
both to feed on your body and to become your body.
Forgive our sins, sustain our faith, and unite us to you,
that our flesh will be subdued to the spirit,
as we follow you in new obedience. [480]

p. 155.2, Gallican

O God,
Bread of our life,
look on us.
Be the Guardian of our bodies.
Be the Savior of our souls. [481]

p. 155.3, Gallican

We believe that we have received from the holy altar
the body and blood of Christ, our Lord and God.
Therefore we pray to the unity of the blessed Trinity,
that in fullness of faith we may always
hunger and thirst for righteousness,
be strengthened with the grace of this saving food,
and do his work,
that we may hold on to the sacrament we have received,
not for judgment, but for healing;
through our Lord Jesus Christ. [482]

p. 155.4, Gallican

O Lord my God,
Father, Son, and Holy Spirit,
make me always seek and love you,
and through this Holy Communion I have received
may I never depart from you;
for you are God, and beside you there is none else,
forever and ever. [483]

p. 156.1, Mozarabic

O Lord,
we have tasted your perfect sweetness.
May it always give us
forgiveness of sins and health of soul;
through your mercy, O our God,
you are blessed,
and live and govern all things,
now and forever. [484]

p. 156.2, Mozarabic

We have received the cup of the Lord's Passion
and tasted the sweetness of his most holy body.
Let us give thanks and praise to him
and walk in his house with joy and gladness. [485]

p. 156.3, Mozarabic

We have received the body of Christ, and drunk his blood.
We will fear no evil, for the Lord is with us.
May your blood always be life to us,
and salvation of our souls,
O our God. [486]

p. 156.4, Ambrosian

Lord our God,
mercifully keep us
who have received the body and blood of your only Son
far from the blindness of unfaithful disciples,

since we confess and worship Christ our Lord,
true God and fully human.[52] [487]

p. 156.5, Ambrosian

O Lord,
preserve in us the gift of your grace,
that by the power and virtue of the Eucharist
we may be strengthened against all evils of this life
and prepared for the life to come.[53] [488]

p. 156.6, Missal of Matthias Flaccus Illyricus, 1557

I give you thanks, O Lord,
holy Father, almighty, eternal God,
for you have refreshed me
with the most holy body and blood
of your Son, Jesus Christ our Lord.
I pray that this sacrament of our salvation,
which I, an unworthy sinner, have received,
may not be to my judgment or condemnation as I deserve,
but to the profit of my body and soul
to life eternal. [489]

p. 157.1, Sarum

Lord Jesus Christ,
almighty and eternal God,
be merciful to me, and forgive my sins
through your body and blood.
For you have said,
"Whoever feeds on my flesh and drinks my blood
abides in me, and I in him."[54]
Therefore, create in me a clean heart,
and renew a right spirit within me,
and uphold me with your free Spirit,
and cleanse me from all vices and the crafts of the devil,
that I may partake of your heavenly joys;
you live and reign
with the Father and the Holy Spirit,
one God, now and forever. [490]

p. 157.2, Sarum

---

[52] This prayer's reference to the "unfaithful disciples." seems to be referring to an Arian or Nestorian doctrinal controversy about the nature of Christ.

[53] Original translation: "and of the life to come."

[54] John 6:56. Jesus' bread of life discourse is commonly associated with the Lord's Supper, yet in that chapter, Jesus spoke of himself as the bread of life to emphasize our need for him to give and sustain spiritual life, and that we need to take him in completely. John 6 does not refer specifically to the Lord's Supper because the events of John 6 took place about a year before he instituted it.

O Lord,
make this Holy Communion my guide
and my food for the journey
to the haven of eternal salvation.
Let it comfort me when I am harassed by thoughts,
and be a source of sweetest love in good times,
patience in trouble and hardship,
and medicine in sickness.
By this most holy sacrament
give me right faith,
firm hope, perfect love,
strength to renounce the world,
pure desires,
inward peace,
fervent love for you,
a reminder of the Passion of your beloved Son,
and grace to keep my life full of virtue
in your praise and sincere faith.
When my last hour comes,
please give the gift of this great sacrament
with true faith, certain hope, and sincere love,
that I may see you without end. [491]

p. 157.3, Sarum

8.   For a Friend.[55]

O Lord,
may your sacrament be my cleansing,
and deliver your servant _____ from all sin
that *he* may rejoice in the fullness of your heavenly remedy;
through Jesus Christ our Lord. [492]

p. 158.1, Gregorian

O Lord,
by this sacrament
always protect your servant _____,
that *he* may serve you with an undistracted mind
and be free from fear of evil under your shelter;
through Jesus Christ our Lord. [493]

p. 158.2, from two Gregorian prayers

---

[55] These prayers may be prayed for other people who are also receiving the body and blood of Christ.
The following two prayers seem to come from the practice of having masses said for other people, living
or dead.

BAPTISMAL PRAYERS

O God,
you restore human nature
and renew your image in us.[56]
Look on this wonderful sacrament of love,
and continue to give your grace and blessing
to those you have renewed by the washing of regeneration;
through Jesus Christ our Lord. [494]

p. 159.1, Gelasian

O God,
you open the kingdom of heaven
only to those who are born again
of water and the Holy Spirit.
Increase the gifts of your grace on your servants
that those who have been cleansed from all sins
may receive what you have promised;
through our Lord Jesus Christ. [495]

p. 159.2, Gelasian

O God,
you have renewed those who believe in you in the font of baptism.
Preserve those who are born again in Christ in your grace
that they may not lose your blessing
by any incursion of error;
through the same Jesus Christ our Lord. [496]

p. 159.3, Gelasian

O God,
you restore us to eternal life by Christ's resurrection.
Bring this wonderful sacrament of your love to fulfillment
when our Savior comes in his majesty,
as you have given us new birth in baptism,
clothe us with a blessed immortality;
through the same Jesus Christ our Lord. [497]

p. 160.1, Gelasian

O God,
you give us your redemption,
and adopt us as your own.
Look on the works of your mercy,
that those who are born again in Christ
may be given an eternal inheritance and true freedom;
through the same Jesus Christ our Lord. [498]

p. 160.2, Gelasian

---

[56] Original translation: "human nature to a higher than its original dignity,"

121

Almighty and eternal God,
bring us to the fellowship of heavenly joys,
and open your kingdom
to those who are born again of the Holy Spirit,
that the lowly flock may reach that place
where their mighty Shepherd has gone before;
through the same Jesus Christ our Lord. [499]

p. 160.3, Gelasian

O almighty God, hear us.
As you have given your family the perfect grace of baptism,
move our hearts to thoughts of eternal bliss;
through Jesus Christ our Lord. [500]

p. 160.4, Gelasian

O God,
by the Baptism of your only Son
you sanctified the streams of water.
Grant that we who are born again of water and the Spirit
may also receive eternal joys;
through the same Jesus Christ our Lord. [501]

p. 161.1, Gregorian

O Lord,
protect your servants who have been called to your grace.
Since they have been born again in divine baptism
never let them be plucked away
from the power of your kingdom;
through Jesus Christ our Lord. [502]

p. 161.2, Gothic

O God,
you give us your redemption and adoption.
Lift the hearts of your believing people to yourself
that all who have been born again in holy baptism
may understand the mysteries they have received;
through Jesus Christ our Lord. [503]

p. 161.3, Old Gallican

Lord God almighty,
you have commanded your servants
to be born again of water and the Holy Spirit.
Preserve in them the holy baptism they have received
and complete it for the hallowing of your name,
that your grace may always increase in them,
and what they have already received as your gift
they may guard by living a new life. [504]

p. 161.4, Gallican Sacramentary

O God,
by holy Baptism you have given your servant
redemption from *his* sins and a life of rebirth.
O Lord God,
let your face shine on *his* heart forever.
Give *him* the shield of faith
to keep *him* safe from the stealthy attack of all enemies.
Clothe *him* in the robe of your innocence, clean and unpolluted.
Give *him* your Spirit as the seal of your grace, free and pure,
and your guarantee of reconciliation to *him* and us
in your boundless mercy;
for blessed and glorified
is your holy and majestic name,
of Father, Son, and Holy Spirit,
now and ever, and to ages of ages. Amen. [505]

p. 162.1, from the Baptismal Rites of the Eastern Church

O Lord our God, our Master,
by the font of baptism
you enlighten the baptized with heavenly light.
By water and the Spirit you have given your servant
forgiveness of all sins—voluntary and involuntary.
Lay your mighty hand on *him*,
and protect *him* by the power of your goodness.
preserve *him* from losing the guarantee of glory,
and bring *him* to eternal life
and to your good pleasure;
for you are our sanctification,
and to you we render glory,
Father, Son, and Holy Spirit,
now and ever, and to ages of ages. Amen. [506]

p. 162.2, from the Baptismal Rites of the Eastern Church

Preserve those who have put on Christ our God,
and give them victory as they wrestle
against the assaults of all adversaries.
Grant that all who are adorned
with the crown of righteousness
that does not perish
may be victorious even to the end.
For you pity and save,
and to you we give glory,
with your unbegotten Father,
and your most holy, good, and life-giving Spirit,
now and ever, and to ages of ages, Amen. [507]

p. 163.1, from the Baptismal Rites of the Eastern Church

PRAYERS FOR SEVERAL OCCASIONS

1. *For the New Year.*

May Christ our Lord,
who is the Head of every beginning,
give us faithful hearts throughout the coming year
that we may be pleasing in his loving eyes.
O God, you never change as the years pass.
Give us devoted hearts to serve you this year.
Fill the earth with fruitful harvests.
Keep our bodies free from disease,
our souls free from offences,
our lives free from scandals,
and keep all trouble from our borders;
through Jesus Christ your Son our Lord. [508]

p. 164.1, Mozarabic

2. *Dedication or Opening of a Church*

O God of all sanctification,
almighty Sovereign,
your goodness is infinite.
O God,
you are present through all things in heaven and earth,
keeping your mercy for your people who walk in your glory.
Hear the prayers of your servants,
that your eyes may be on this house day and night.
Graciously dedicate this church.
Mercifully enlighten and brighten it with your own glory.
Favorably receive everyone who comes to worship in this place.
Graciously listen to those who pray in this holy house.
By your great name and mighty hand,
always protect, hear, keep and defend them.
Give them your constant happiness
that they may always rejoice in your true religion
and persevere in the Christian faith of the Holy Trinity;
through Jesus Christ our Lord. [509]

p. 164.2, Gelasian

O God,
although you are present everywhere,
and fill all things with your majesty,
yet you make yourself known
in places consecrated to you,
and houses of prayer
move the hearts of your people to call on your name.
Pour out your grace on this place

and show your gracious help to all who hope in you,
that here they may receive both the power of your Sacraments
and the answer to their prayers;
through Jesus Christ our Lord. [510]

p. 165.1, Gelasian

O God,
you are the Author of all gifts
which are consecrated to you.
Be with us as we dedicate this place,
that those who have built it in honor of your name
may have you as their Protector in all things;
through Jesus Christ our Lord. [511]

p. 165.2, Gelasian

O almighty God,
grant that in this place we dedicate to your name
you would graciously listen to all who seek you;
through Jesus Christ our Lord. [512]

p. 166.1, Gregorian

O Lord,
may our prayers please you,
and may all who enter this temple
(of which we celebrate the anniversary of its dedication)
please you with full and complete devotion of soul and body.
As we pray to you, help us,
so that we receive your eternal rewards;
through our Lord Jesus Christ. [513]

p. 166.2, Gregorian

O God,
you are building for yourself
an eternal dwelling out of living and chosen stones.
Help your people,
that as your Church grows with buildings and with numbers,
it may also be grow spiritually;
through Jesus Christ our Lord. [514]

p. 166.3, Gregorian

3. In Time of War.

Almighty and merciful God,
give us rest from the storm of war.
You will give us all good things
when you give us peace of soul and body;
through Jesus Christ our Lord. [515]

p. 167.1, Leonine

O God our Defender,
look on us and protect us from fear of the enemy.
Remove all disturbances
that we may serve you with minds free from distraction;
through Jesus Christ our Lord. [516]

p. 167.2, Leonine

O Lord,
be gracious to us in our times.
In your goodness,
maintain both national quietness and Christian devotion;
through Jesus Christ our Lord. [517]

p. 167.3, Leonine

Almighty and eternal God,
crush the force of our enemies
so that we may celebrate your holy service
with undisturbed minds;
through Jesus Christ our Lord. [518]

p. 167.4, Leonine

O Lord,
let the invincible defense of your power
be the fortress of your faithful people.
Free them from the assault of enemies
that they may be devoted to you with holy love
and always persevere in your grace;
through Jesus Christ our Lord. [519]

p. 167.5, Gelasian

O God,
Maker of the universe,
the course of the world proceeds by your command.
Hear our prayers
and give us now the tranquility of peace
that we may continually rejoice in your mercy;
through Jesus Christ our Lord. [520]

p. 168.1, Gelasian

4.   In Time of Pestilence or any Affliction.

O Lord,
look mercifully on the affliction of your people.
Do not let our sins destroy us,
but let your abundant mercy prevail in saving us;
through Jesus Christ our Lord. [521]

p. 168.2, Leonine

O God,
you do not desire the death of sinners,
but that they return to you and live.
In your mercy, turn your people to yourself.
When they devote themselves to you
remove the scourges of your anger;
through Jesus Christ our Lord. [522]

p. 168.3, Gelasian

O Lord,
mercifully drive the destructive fury of disease
away from your faithful people,
together with their own errors.
As you discipline them when they go astray,
protect them with your pity when they are brought back;
through Jesus Christ our Lord. [523]

p. 168.4, Gelasian

O Lord,
answer our prayers
and mercifully turn away the famine (*or* the pestilence),
that people may know
that these scourges both proceed from your righteous anger
and cease by your compassion;
through Jesus Christ our Lord. [524]

p. 169.1, Gelasian

Almighty God,
with Fatherly tenderness
receive those who flee from your anger,
that those who dread the scourge that comes from your majesty
may rejoice in your forgiveness;
through Jesus Christ our Lord. [525]

p. 169.2, Gelasian

O Lord,
receive our prayers,
and do not enter into judgment with your servants.
No righteousness is found in us on which we could rely,
so we trust in you, the Fountain of pity,
both to be cleansed from our sins
and delivered from our distresses;
through Jesus Christ our Lord. [526]

p. 169.3, Gelasian

O God,
your loving-kindness surpasses understanding,
since the conversion of one sinner
causes great rejoicing in heaven.
Look on this small portion of your people,
that all affliction may be removed,
and your inheritance may increase in numbers
and advance in devotion;
through Jesus Christ our Lord. [527]

p. 169.4, Gelasian

O Lord,
in your compassion,
turn away the wrath we deserve for our sins,
but because of our human frailty we cannot endure.
Embrace us with that tenderness you give to the unworthy;
through Jesus Christ our Lord. [528]

p. 170.1, Gelasian

O God,
you discipline us in love
to cleanse us from our iniquities.
Help us learn from your discipline,
and rejoice in your comfort. [529]

p. 170.2, Gregorian

O Lord,
we praise you at all times.
When you rebuke us, it is in mercy,
when you correct us with discipline,
when you hold us near with forgiveness,
when you heal us with chastening,
and strengthen us with healing.
May we who have tasted your sweetness by faith
enjoy the fullness of your delights in the day your return;
through your mercy, O our God,
you are blessed,
and live and govern all things,
now and forever. [530]

p. 170.3, Mozarabic

O kind Master,
spare and forgive us.
Withhold the scourge that we deserve.
Let your great compassion overcome our many sins.
Let the depths of your infinite goodness
cover the bitter sea of our wickedness.
We have examples of your kindness

to robbers, harlots, tax collectors, and the prodigal son.
Like them,
we also make our confession to you and fall before you.
Receive us, O Master.
Although we fall far short of the glory of God,
let your infinite goodness cover every defect.
Every scourge and plague,
and every form of destruction, which bears down on us,
is slight and small in comparison
with our innumerable transgressions.
Therefore, because of our many sins
we have no ground of confidence,
O Lord, righteous Judge,
to request of your goodness a relief from this terrible menace, —
except your exceedingly great tenderness
and the depths of your compassion.
O Master full of pity,
let your mercy compel us
to ask for what is beyond our deserving.
O God of exceeding goodness, O Lord of mercy,
we humbly ask you to hold back the sharp sword of untimely death.
O kind Lord,
accept our contrition and heart-felt sorrow,
as you accepted the tears of Hezekiah in the sorrow of his heart
and rescued him from death.
Remember, O serene One,
the cross and death and voluntary passion you endured for us
to take our condemnation.
From you alone
we beg assistance and relief from these horrors.
With you alone are possible
the things which are impossible with man.
Blessed are you forever. [531]

p. 171.1, Eastern Church Office, time of pestilence

O Lord of exceeding goodness,
Maker of the universe,
your mercy is immeasurable,
your kindness is incomprehensible.
You took away all our iniquities
and nailed them to your cross,
so that you, the sinless One,
might sanctify us.
We fall before you in humble prayer,
O patient Lord,
and looking on the depths of your wonderful kindness,

we cry to you, our Lord.
Save us.
We offer you our worship
not in the spirit of the Pharisee
but in the spirit of the tax collector,
We do not imitate the mocking thief
but the humble one who confessed his sin and turned to you.
We cry to you with the prayer,
"Remember. Remember us, O Lord,
in mercy and compassion."
Send down to us your holy guardian angel
to whom you have entrusted our lives,
that he may rescue us from this terrible raging death,
and through your deliverance and release
we may glorify you. [57] [532]

p. 172.1, Eastern Church Prayers in time of public calamity

5. *Thanksgiving on Removal of Calamities.*

Almighty and eternal God,
you heal us by chastening
and preserve us by pardoning.
Let us rejoice in the comfort
of the tranquility we desired,
and use the gift of your peace
for the true amendment of our lives;
through Jesus Christ our Lord. [533]

p. 173.1, Leonine

O Lord,
we must shout your praises.
By releasing us from the evils we deserved,
you enable us to celebrate your good gifts with gladness;
through Jesus Christ our Lord. [534]

p. 173.2, Leonine

O Lord,
we thank you for relieving us
from the pressure of temporal affliction,
that you may set us forward
on the way to eternal joys;
through Jesus Christ our Lord. [535]

p. 173.3, Leonine

---

[57] Some lines were omitted in the revision to avoid redundancy and improve the flow of the prayer.
Parts of this revision are a freer paraphrase.

We plead for your mercy with our whole heart,
that as you defend us against things that harm body,
set us free from the enemies of the soul.
As you let us rejoice in outward tranquility,
give us your inward peace;
through Jesus Christ our Lord. [536]

p. 173.4, Leonine

O Lord our God,
do not let the relief from anxiety
your mercy has given us
make us negligent,
but rather cause us to become
more acceptable worshipers of your name;
through Jesus Christ our Lord. [537]

p. 174.1, Leonine

O Lord,
as you have delivered us from impending dangers,
graciously absolve us from our sins.
Make us obedient to your commands
that you may bestow on us greater benefits;
through Jesus Christ our Lord. [538]

p. 174.2, Leonine

6. For a Blessing on Social Interactions.

O God,
you visit the humble
and comfort us with the love of our friends.
Graciously bless our fellowship,
that through those in whom you dwell,
we may feel that you have come to visit us;
through Jesus Christ our Lord. [539]

p. 175.2, Gelasian / Gregorian

O God,
you show us signs of your presence.
Pour on us the Spirit of love,
that with the presence of our friends and coworkers
we may be blessed by your bountiful grace;
through Jesus Christ our Lord. [540]

p. 175.1, Gelasian

7. *Before and after Meals.*

Bless, O Lord, your gifts
we are about to receive
from your goodness.
May your gifts, Lord,
be our refreshment,
and your grace our comfort;
through Jesus Christ our Lord. [541]

p. 175.2, Gelasian

We have been satisfied, O Lord,
with your gifts and blessings.
Fill us with your mercy.
You are blessed,
and with the Father and the Holy Spirit,
you live and reign, one God, now and forever. [542]

p. 175.3, Gelasian

PRAYERS FOR THE USE OF THE CLERGY

1.   For Deacons.

O Lord our God,
you pour out your Holy Spirit
on those you have set apart
to be stewards of your mysteries.
Keep your servant
that he may hold the mystery of the faith
in a pure conscience and with all virtue.
Give him the grace given to your first martyr Stephen,
that he may do the work to which he is called.
By your holy and life-giving Spirit,
fill him with all faith and love,
power and sanctification.
For you are our God,
and to you we give glory,
Father, Son, and Holy Spirit,
now and ever,
to ages of ages. [543]

p. 176.1, from two prayers in the Ordinal of the Eastern Church

2.   For Priests.

O God,
you are great in power,
unsearchable in understanding,
and wonderful in your plans for us.
Fill your servant with the gift of the Holy Spirit
that he may stand before your holy altar blameless,
to announce the gospel of your kingdom,
to administer the Word of your truth,
to offer gifts and spiritual sacrifices to you,
and to renew your people in the font of rebirth,
that when your only Son,
our great God and Savior Jesus Christ, comes again,
by your mercies he will receive your reward;
for your holy and majestic name is blessed and glorified. [544]

p. 177.1, Ordinal of the Eastern Church

It is truly good and right
for us to pray to your majesty,
that when our Lord comes
he will find us serving our coworkers.
In our dealings with your people
help us to be careful to balance affection with correction,
and needful rebukes with love,

that we wisely discharge the service committed to us
and not become guilty of failing to put our Lord's deposit to work
but profit from having multiplied God's talents
of which we have been made the stewards. [545]

p. 178.1, Leonine

Almighty God,
grant that we may behave ourselves
in a manner fitting the grace we have received,
and may display to your faithful people
examples of godly conduct,
and that the eternal salvation of your people
may adorn the reward of their shepherd;
through our Lord. [546]

p. 178.3, Leonine

O God,
Creator and Ruler of the world,
hear my humble prayers.
As you have allowed me
to be a steward of your mysteries,
not because of anything I deserve
but out of your infinite goodness,
so make me a fitting minister at your sacred altar;
through Jesus Christ our Lord. [547]

p. 179.1, Leonine

O holy Lord, Father almighty, eternal God,
carry us forward by the gifts of your grace,
and by your Spirit give us
what human weakness cannot achieve.
Establish a strong faith in us
that those who serve at your altars
shine like stars in the sky
as we hold firmly to the word of life;
through Jesus Christ our Lord. [548]

p. 179.3, Leonine, see prayer [335]

Who can be worthy of this office,
unless you prepare him for it
by your all-surrounding grace and compassion?
Since it is your gift
and not something we merit,
you must give us your guidance
that we may not suffer punishment for our negligence,
but do the duty you have given us
and receive your eternal reward;
through Jesus Christ our Lord. [549]

p. 180.2, Leonine

O Lord,
let your gracious light shine on your church
that your flock may go on and prosper everywhere,
and its pastors, by your guidance,
bring glory to your name;[58]
through Jesus Christ our Lord. [550]

p. 180.4, Leonine

O merciful God and eternal King,
bring success to our service.
Watch over your holy flock
that we may be pleasing in your sight
as your people are devoted to you.
Guide the wills of all
to keep your commands. [551]

p. 181.2, Leonine

O merciful and pitying Lord,
you support us by sparing us
and sanctify us by forgiving.
Pardon our sins,
and keep those who serve your heavenly sacraments
free from all offence,
through Jesus Christ our Lord. [552]

p. 181.4, Gelasian

O God,
you tenderly provide for your people
and rule over them in love.
Give the Spirit of wisdom
to those you have called to govern your church
that the holy sheep enjoy well-being
and their pastors always rejoice;
through Jesus Christ our Lord. [553]

p. 182.1, Gregorian

Almighty God,
clothe me in your righteousness,
that I may rejoice with all your saints.
Cleanse me from the stain of sin
and enable me to please you with my service.
Remove the burdens of sin from my conscience,
and by your mercy, preserve me from all vices;
through our Lord Jesus Christ. [554]

p. 182.3, Gregorian

---

[58] Original translation: "may become acceptable to Thy Name;"

O God,
you pass over the sins of human weakness
and call undeserving men to the dignity of the ministry.
Not only do you pardon sins,
but you also justify the sinners themselves.
As a gift, by your power, things that are not have a beginning.
The things begun receive nourishment.
The things receiving nourishment bear fruit.
The things being fruitful are aided to continue.
You created me when I was not.
After you created me, you gave me steadfast faith.
As one of your faithful, a poor sinner, you called me to your service.
I humbly ask your almighty goodness
to cleanse me from past sins,
to strengthen me in good works as I live in this world,
and to give me the power to persevere.
May I serve at your altar
and join the fellowship
of the faithful shepherds of your people.[59]
May my prayer be acceptable to you
by him who offered himself to you as a sacrifice,
the Maker of all things,
and the only High Priest without spot of sin,
Jesus Christ our Lord. [555]

p. 183.2, Gregorian

3. Celebration of the Holy Eucharist.

O God,
Fountain of goodness and Source of kindness,
you do not immediately condemn sinners,
but compassionately wait for their repentance.
Wash away all offences
and prepare me to perform the work you have given me.
Make me worthy and strong
to carry out the service of your altar with trembling hands,
and be justified with all your saints;
through Jesus Christ our Lord. [556]

p. 185.1, Gregorian

O most merciful God,
incline your loving ears to my prayers
and enlighten my heart with the grace of the Holy Spirit,
that I may worthily administer your sacraments,
love you with an everlasting love,

---

[59] Original translation: "And make me so to serve Thine altars, that I may be able to attain the fellowship of those priests who have been pleasing to Thee."

136

and be received to everlasting joys;
through Jesus Christ our Lord. [557]

p. 185.3, York Missal

We give you thanks,
O Lord, God of hosts,
for receiving our service at your holy altar.
We ask your mercy to forgive our sins
and the errors of your people.
O Lord, hear our prayer.
Prepare us to offer our supplications and prayers to you
and the sacrament of the altar to all your people.
By the power of your Holy Spirit,
enable us to keep our conscience pure
and call on you in every time and place. [558]

p. 185.4, Liturgy of St. Chrysostom

O Lord God,
Father almighty,
bless and sanctify our prayer and praise[60]
which has been offered to you,
to the honor and glory of your name,
and pardon the sins of your people,
and hear my prayer,
and forgive me all my sins;
through Christ our Lord. [559]

p. 186.1, Mozarabic Missal

O Lord Jesus Christ, our God,
hear from your holy dwelling
and from the glorious throne of your kingdom,
and sanctify us.
You sit above with the Father
but are invisibly present with us.
Give your immaculate body and your precious blood to us
and to all your people. [560]

p. 187.1, Liturgy of St. Chrysostom

O Lord,
we rejoice in the richness of your gifts.
As you have given us power to hold this ministry
give us sufficient grace to fulfil it;
through our Lord. [561]

p. 187.3, Leonine

---

[60] Original translation: "our sacrifice of praise."

O Lord,
as I receive this sacrament,
erase the stains of my sins,
and empower me to carry out the office you have given me;
through our Lord. [562]

p. 187.5, Gregorian

Going from strength to strength,
and having finished the Divine Service in your temple,
O Lord our God,
let us enjoy your perfect love. [563]

p. 188.1, Liturgy of St. James

4. Baptism and other Ordinances.

O God,
by your invisible power
you wonderfully give power to your sacraments.
Although we are unworthy to perform such great mysteries,
you make us stewards of the gifts of your grace.[61]
Listen to our prayers.
Be with us in your goodness.
Assist us in your loving-kindness
while we keep your commands,
O God Almighty. [564]

p. 188.3, Gelasian, consecration of the Font, Easter Eve

May what we are to do in our humble service,
be completed by your effectual power. [565]

p. 189.1, Gelasian

O Lord,
hear our prayers,
and graciously listen to me,
the first to need your mercy.
You have made me a minister of this work,
not by choosing me because of merit
but by the gift of your grace,
so give me confidence to perform your ministry
and carry out the act of your own loving-kindness;
through our Lord. [566]

p. 189.3, Gelasian, Prayer over Penitents on Maundy Thursday

Be present,
O merciful God,
that what has been done by our ministry and service

---

[61] Original translation: "and although we be unworthy to perform such great mysteries, yet Thou forsakest not the gifts of Thy grace,"

may be confirmed by your blessing;
through our Lord. [567]

p. 189.5, Leonine

5.   Preaching.

Almighty and eternal God,
you are the source and perfection of all virtues.
Help us do what is right and preach what is true,
that by action and teaching
we may instruct your faithful people in your grace;
through Jesus Christ our Lord. [568]

p. 190.2, Leonine

6.   Visitation.

Hear us,
holy Lord, Father almighty, eternal God,
and join the grace of your own visitation to our humble services,
that you may make yourself a dwelling
in the hearts of those whose dwelling we visit;
through Jesus Christ our Lord. [569]

p. 190.4, Gelasian

O God,
you are the protector of the faithful
and constant visitor of those obedient to you.
Be present and merciful
to your servants who dwell in this house,
that while we visit them
you may guard them with divine favor;
through our Lord. [570]

p. 191.2, Gelasian

O Lord,
bless this house and all who dwell in it,
as you were pleased to bless the tents
of Abraham, Isaac and Jacob,
that within these walls may dwell an angel of light,
and that those who dwell together in it
may receive your heavenly blessing like abundant dew,
and through your tenderness rejoice in peace and quiet;
through Jesus Christ our Lord. [571]

p. 191.4, Gelasian

Almighty and merciful God,
you use the work of your ministers
for the giving of service and prayer to you.
In your boundless mercy, we ask
that whatever we visit, you would visit,
that whatever we bless, you would bless,
and when we enter, evil spirits may flee away,
and the angel of peace may come in;
through Jesus Christ our Lord. [572]

p. 192.2, Gregorian

Almighty and merciful God,
in your boundless loving-kindness,
save your servant _____, who is lying in this house,
weary with sickness. [573]

p. 193.1, Rheims manuscript / Menard

May the Father,
who created all things in the beginning, bless you.
May the Son of God heal you.
May the Holy Spirit enlighten you,
guard your body, save your soul,
direct your thoughts,
and bring you safe to the heavenly country,
where he lives and reigns,
God, in a perfect Trinity,
forever and ever. [574]

p. 193.2, Sarum

May our Lord Jesus Christ
be near you to defend you,
within you to refresh you,
around you to preserve you,
before you to guide you,
behind you to justify you,
above you to bless you;
who lives and reigns
with the Father and the Holy Spirit,
one God, now and forever. [575]

p. 193.3, 10th C. manuscript / Menard

7.   Anniversary of Ordination.

O God,
by your command the order of all time runs its course.
Look graciously on me your servant,
whom you have called into your ministry.
Mercifully preserve your gifts in me

so that my service may be pleasing to you;
through Jesus Christ our Lord. [576]

p. 194.1, Gelasian

8.   *Prayer for the Flock.*

I have no confidence in anything but your mercy,
so give my mouth power to proclaim your truth,
and sanctify my work with the abundant riches of your grace,
that you may both save me
and in your loving-kindness, justify the flock entrusted to me.
Whatever you see corrupt in them, make sound.
Whatever you discern as defective in me, cure,
Whatever guilt they have earned through my
    sinful luke-warmness or carelessness, put away.
If they have fallen into sin, with or without my knowledge,
    or have fallen by the stumbling block of my example, pardon them.
Do not give me the punishment I would deserve for that.
Let the rebukes I have given others lead to their repentance.
Hear the pleading of this prayer and recall them from the error they
    have committed.
Pardon their iniquities, that they may not endure the torments of hell.
Wash away my sins and my guilt, and purify my unworthy service.
Incline your ear, O God, to our prayers,
and write me, and those who are committed to me, in your books,
that I, together with the flock entrusted to me,
cleansed from all sin,
may be enabled to depart to you in peace. [577]

p. 195.1, from an "Apologia Sacerdotis" in Menard's Gregorian

O Christ,
look down from heaven on your flock and lambs
and bless their bodies and souls.
O Christ,
grant those who have received your sign on their foreheads
remain your own in the day of judgment. [578]

p. 196.2, Pontificale of Egbert

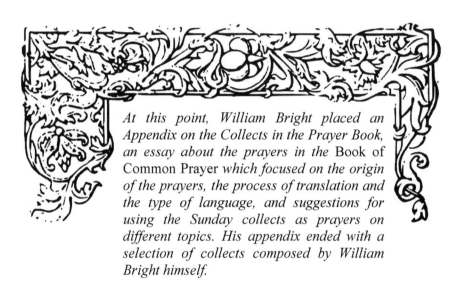

At this point, William Bright placed an Appendix on the Collects in the Prayer Book, an essay about the prayers in the Book of Common Prayer *which focused on the origin of the prayers, the process of translation and the type of language, and suggestions for using the Sunday collects as prayers on different topics. His appendix ended with a selection of collects composed by William Bright himself.*

PRAYERS FROM THE END OF THE APPENDIX TO BRIGHT'S *ANCIENT COLLECTS*

I venture to place here, by themselves, a few Collects constructed in imitation of the ancient model.

[*William Bright*]

For the Spirit of Prayer.
Almighty God,
every good prayer comes from you,
and you pour out the Spirit of grace and prayer
on all who desire it.
Deliver us from cold hearts
and wandering minds
when we draw near you,
that with steadfast thoughts
and warmed affections
we may worship you in spirit and in truth;
through Jesus Christ our Lord. [579]

p. 233.6, William Bright

Sunday Morning.
O God,
you make us glad
with the weekly remembrance
of your Son's resurrection.
Bless us today as we worship you,
that we may enjoy your favor
in the week ahead;
through Jesus Christ our Lord. [580]

p. 233.7, William Bright

Sunday Evening.
O Lord,
you triumphed over the powers of darkness
and prepared our place in the New Jerusalem.
As we have given thanks for your resurrection today,
may we also praise you in that city
where you are the light;
where with the Father and the Holy Spirit
you live and reign,
one God, now and forever. [581]

p. 234.1, William Bright

Before Study of Scripture.
O Lord Jesus Christ,
you are truth incarnate and the teacher of the faithful.
Send your Holy Spirit as we read your Word,
and transform our thoughts as we read what you reveal,
that as we learn about you with honest hearts,
we may be rooted and built up in you;
who live and reign with your Father and the Holy Spirit,
one God, now and forever. [582]

p. 234.2, William Bright

For Guidance.
O God,
with your judgment you guide the humble,
and your light shines in the darkness on those who do not know you.
Move us to ask you what to do
when we have doubts and uncertainty,
that the Spirit of wisdom
may save us from all wrong choices,
and in your light, we may see light,
and not stumble from your straight path;
through Jesus Christ our Lord. [583]

p. 234.3, William Bright

For Cheerfulness.
O most loving Father,
you want us to give thanks for all things,
to dread nothing but losing you,
and to cast all our anxiety on you
because you care for us.
Preserve us from faithless fears and worldly anxieties
and grant that no clouds of this mortal life
may hide from us the light of that love
which is immortal,
and which you have shown us
in your Son, Jesus Christ our Lord. [584]

p.234.4, William Bright

For Grace to Speak the Truth in Love.
O Lord and Savior Jesus Christ,
you did not come to quarrel or cry aloud,
but to let your words fall as the rain waters the earth.
May all who contend for the faith
never injure it by discord and impatience,
but speaking your precious truth in love,
present it that it may be loved,

and that people may see your truth
as goodness and beauty. [585]

p. 235.1, William Bright

Against Spiritual Apathy.
O God,
good and gracious King of our souls,
you want to rule in the hearts of all your children.
Deliver us from laziness in doing your work
and all coldness from following your will.
Rekindle our love when we look to you
and renew our strength as we wait for you;
through Jesus Christ our Lord. [586]

p. 236.3, William Bright

For Hatred of Sin.
O God,
no one can love you
unless they also hate what is evil.
You sent your Son, our Savior,
to redeem us from all our iniquities.
Deliver us when we look at sin without despising it.
Let the power of his passion
come between us and the enemy of our souls;
through Jesus Christ our Lord. [587]

p. 236.3, William Bright

On the Incarnation.
We adore you, blessed Jesus,
true God, yet fully human,
you are the same
yesterday, today and forever,
our mighty Salvation,
our only Hope.
Keep us in your care,
now and in the hour of our death.
Keep us faithful to you while we live on earth
and blessed with you in heaven;
where with the Father and the Holy Spirit
you live and reign,
one God, now and forever. [588]

p. 236.1, William Bright

145

On the Example of the Blessed Virgin.
O Christ, God Incarnate,
your mother was blessed in bearing you
but even more blessed in keeping your Word.
May we who remember her humility
follow the example
of her devotion to do your will;
you live and reign,
with the Father and the Holy Spirit
one God, now and forever. [589]

p. 236.2, William Bright

On the Communion of Saints.
O God,
you have gathered us
to a host of angels that no one can count,
and to the spirits of righteous people
made complete in you.
Help us remain in their fellowship
even during our pilgrimage on earth
and finally make us share in their joy
in the heavenly country;
through Jesus Christ our Lord. [590]

p. 236.3, William Bright

For a Friend.
Good Lord Jesus,
I give you thanks
for all you have given me
through your servant _____.
Bless him
in ways immeasurably more
than I could ask or imagine.
Help us to love each other in you and for you,
to be one in heart,
even though separated by distance and time,
and to walk as friends as we serve you.
Finally, unite us forever before your throne, at your feet,
where peace and love are perfect and unending,
and you, with the Father and the Holy Spirit
live and rule,
one God, now and forever. [591]

p. 236.4, William Bright

For the Clergy.
O Lord,
bless all your clergy

146

that they may handle your holy things with holiness,
and be pleasing to you,
our Priest forever. [592]

p. 237.1, William Bright

For All Who Do the Work of the Church.
O Lord,
without you, our best work is a loss,
and with you, the weak can go forth like the mighty.
Watch over all the works in your church
done according to your will.
Give your workers
pure intentions,
patient faith,
some successes on earth,
and the bliss of serving you in heaven;
through Jesus Christ our Lord. [593]

p. 237.2, William Bright

For Sufferers.
Lord Jesus Christ, our Savior,
for us you bore the agony of the cross.
Draw near to your servant _____,
who suffers *pain in body or trouble of mind.*
Make all *his* crosses serve your holy purpose,
and after this life,
Crown *him* in your kingdom
where all tears are wiped away;
with the Father and the Holy Spirit
you live and reign,
one God, now and forever. [594]

p. 237.3, William Bright

Lord Jesus Christ, our Savior,
for us you bore the agony of the cross.
Draw near to your servant _____,
who suffers *pain in body or trouble of mind,*
and make all things serve your good purpose,
that by your grace *he* may know
that the sufferings of this present time
are not worth comparing
with the glory that is to be revealed to us;
with the Father and the Holy Spirit
you live and reign,
one God, now and forever. [595]

p. 237.3, William Bright and Paul C. Stratman

For the Tempted.
Lord Jesus,
our merciful and faithful High Priest,
for us you were tempted by Satan.
Help your servants
who are attacked by many temptations.
You know their weakness.
Let each one know your power to save;
for you live and reign with the Father and the Holy Spirit,
One God, now and forever. [596]

p. 237.4, William Bright

For Those Who Live in Sin.
O compassionate Father,
have mercy on all who are hardened
by the deceitfulness of sin.
Give them your grace
and the will and power to return to you,
and the loving welcome of your forgiveness;
through Jesus Christ our Lord. [597]

p. 238.1, William Bright

For Those Who Stray from the Faith.
Almighty and eternal God,
you have given us the Christian faith from Christ
to be a lamp for our feet in the darkness of this world.
Have pity on all who have gone astray from your safe paths
by doubting or denying it.
Bring your truth home to their hearts,
and move them to receive it as little children;
through Jesus Christ our Lord. [598]

p. 238.2, William Bright

Printed in Great Britain
by Amazon